You Don't Need JavaScript

A practical guide to creating modern websites and interfaces using only CSS

Theo Soti

<packt>

You Don't Need JavaScript

Portfolio Director: Ashwin Nair
Portfolio Manager: Bhavya Rao
Project Manager: Ruvika Rao
Content Engineer: Nisha Cleetus
Technical Editor: Rohit Singh
Indexer: Pratik Shirodkar
Production Designer: Ponraj Dhandapani
Growth Lead: Anamika Singh

First published: June 2026

Production reference: 2180626

Published by Packt Publishing Ltd.
Grosvenor House
11 St Paul's Square
Birmingham
B3 1RB, UK.

ISBN 978-1-80778-341-9
`www.packtpub.com`

About the author

Theo Soti is a frontend developer, writer, and educator focused on modern CSS, semantic HTML, and building lighter web experiences. Through practical experiments and real interface patterns, he helps developers question JavaScript-first habits and make better use of the platform. His work centers on accessibility, performance, and progressive enhancement, with a clear goal: helping teams build websites that are faster, and more resilient.

Table of Contents

Preface xi

Part 1: Everyday Features 1

Chapter 1: Conditionally Styling with :has() 3

Understanding :has() 3
Practical Use Cases 3
Styling based on form input • 4
Conditional Styles for Navigation • 4
Advanced Combinations • 5
Checking adjacent siblings • 7
Changing layouts with a toggle • 7
Browser Support and Fallbacks 9

Chapter 2: Dark Mode in CSS 11

Detecting the System Preference 12
The light-dark() Helper Function 13
Adding a User Toggle 14
Persisting User Choice with localStorage 16

Chapter 3: Smooth Scrolling to Sections 19

Smooth scrolling 19
Smooth scrolling in scrollable containers 20
Handling fixed headers 20
Option A - Global offset • 20
Option B - Per-element offset • 21

Chapter 4: Native Modals with <dialog> 23

The Basic HTML Structure 24
Opening the Dialog with JavaScript 25
Animating the Dialog 25
Styling the Backdrop 26

Chapter 5: Accordions with Pure CSS 29

The Basic HTML Structure 29
Linking Multiple Accordions with name 30
Showing Content by Default with open 30
Built-In Find-in-Page Support (Ctrl + F / Cmd + F) 31
Hiding the Default Triangle 31
Custom Arrow with :after 32
Smooth Content Animation 32
Complementary Native Features 34

Chapter 6: Pure-CSS Automatic Slider 37

The Basic HTML Structure 38
The Slider Container 39
Animating the Items 39
Pausing on Hover and Focus 41

Chapter 7: Auto-Numbered Headings 43

The Basic HTML Structure 44
Numbering top-level headings 45
Numbering nested sub-headings 46
Variations and styles 48

Chapter 8: Other Use-Case of Counter 49

The Basic HTML 49
Making a custom property animatable 50

Driving the count with keyframes 50
Print the counter 51
Putting it all together 51
Respecting reduced motion 52

Part 2: Modern CSS Power Moves 55

Chapter 9: Custom Border Animations 57

The Basic HTML Structure 58
Preparing the card 58
Adding a border layer 59
Declaring an animatable property 60
Drawing the gradient 60
Animating the spin 61
Adding the glow 62
Respecting reduced motion 63

Chapter 10: View Transitions 65

HTML structure 66
Opting into transitions 67
Choosing what animates 67
Styling the snapshots 67
Defining the motion 68
Respect reduced-motion 68

Chapter 11: CSS Motion Path 71

The Basic HTML Structure 71
Draw the route 72
Make the Container Match the SVG dimensions 73
Draw the square 74
Give it a path to follow 74
Animate along the curve 75

Optional Path Visibility 76
Accessibility 77
Troubleshooting 78

Chapter 12: CSS Mask Effects 81

The Basic HTML Structure 81
Stacking everything with grid 82
Complementary masks 83
Styling the slider 84
Updating the divider with JavaScript 85
Accessibility 85
Other use cases 86
Read-only stars rating • 86
Masked banner silhouette • 87

Chapter 13: CSS-Only Form Validation 91

The Basic HTML 92
Base styling and a hidden message list 93
Color by "user" states (only after interaction) 93
Show messages for both classic and "user" validity 94
Always validate on submit 94

Part 3: A Glimpse of the Future 97

Chapter 14: Scroll-Driven Animations 99

The Basic HTML Structure 100
Draw the track 100
Add the fill 100
Define the animation 101
Link animation to scroll 101
Other use cases: 102
Coverflow-on-scroll (horizontal view timeline) • 102

Section image reveal • 103

Chapter 15: Native Popovers 107

The Basic HTML Structure ... 108
Minimal skin (make it look like a card) ... 108
Built-in close control ... 109
Adding animation ... 109
Another Use Case: Off-Canvas Menu • 111

Chapter 16: Customized Selects 115

The Basic HTML Structure ... 116
Opting In ... 117
Styling the Button Face ... 117
Customizing the Arrow ... 118
Styling the Dropdown and Its Options ... 119
Keeping the Button Tidy ... 120
Style the selected option and its checkmark ... 121

Chapter 17: Anchor Positioning 125

The Basic HTML Structure ... 125
Declaring the Anchor ... 126
Associating the Tooltip ... 126
Placing with anchor() ... 127
Avoiding Clipping with Fallbacks ... 127
Matching the Anchor's Width (Optional) ... 128

Chapter 18: Native CSS Carousels 131

The Basic HTML Structure ... 131
Lay out the track ... 132
Add pagination dots ... 133
Add navigation arrows ... 135

Chapter 19: And more to come... 139

Native custom functions and mixins 139
Inline conditionals with if() 140
Masonry-style layout via Item Flow 140
True randomness with random() 141
sibling-index() and sibling-count() 141
More powerful attr() 142
field-sizing (auto-growing form controls) 143

Chapter 20: Closing Thoughts 145

Index 147

Preface

JavaScript is powerful. No argument there. But what if much of what you're solving with JS could be handled just as well, or even better, using modern CSS and semantic HTML? This book is based on a simple principle: use the least powerful tool that gets the job done.

The Rule of Least Power

This principle originates from the philosophy behind web standards: always choose the simplest tool that effectively accomplishes the job. Start with semantic HTML to structure your content, enhance presentation and interactions with CSS, and reach for JavaScript only when absolutely necessary.

HTML and CSS are declarative languages. You describe your intent (the final look and behavior) and the browser determines the most efficient way to execute it. This approach inherently leads to simpler, more maintainable, and more accessible websites. JavaScript, however, is imperative. It demands that you explicitly define every step the browser must take, increasing complexity, performance overhead, and potential points of failure.

Why Do We Default to JavaScript?

It's easy and tempting to reach for JavaScript. Popular frameworks such as React, Vue, and Angular have made rapid prototyping and rich interactivity extremely convenient. While this convenience has significant advantages, it also often leads to bloated bundles, slower load times, and unnecessary complexity.

On the other hand, browsers have significantly evolved. Modern CSS and HTML have caught up remarkably, offering powerful capabilities once reserved solely for JavaScript. You can now implement sophisticated UI patterns such as modals, accordions, carousels, toggles, and animations purely through native browser technologies.

Why it Matters

Using minimal JavaScript translates to leaner codebases, improved accessibility, better performance, and reduced reliance on third-party libraries. Moreover, it results in decreased energy consumption, both for users and servers, significantly lowering your site's environmental footprint.

However, the aim isn't to entirely remove JavaScript. Certain tasks like real-time data fetching, complex business logic, advanced interactivity, will always benefit from JS. The goal is balance: employ JavaScript exactly where it provides genuine value, not simply because it's familiar or convenient.

By embracing a CSS-first approach, you enhance accessibility inherently. Semantic HTML and native browser behaviors are optimized for assistive technologies, supporting a broader audience by default.

Performance and Sustainability

A lighter reliance on JavaScript also means faster initial load times, reduced CPU usage, and less battery drain. For instance, substituting a JavaScript slider library (which typically weighs 50-100KB of minified JS) with a pure CSS implementation reduces overhead and significantly boosts performance.

This book invites you to pause before reaching for JavaScript. Always ask yourself first: Can CSS handle this? You'll find that the answer is "yes" more often than you'd expect, empowering you to build faster, cleaner, and more accessible websites from the start.

In the course of this book, we will cover:

- Conditionally Styling with `:has()`
- Dark Mode in CSS
- Smooth Scrolling to Sections
- Native Modals with `<dialog>`
- Accordions with Pure CSS
- Pure-CSS Automatic Slider
- Auto-Numbered Headings
- Other Use-Case of Counter
- Custom Border Animations
- View Transitions
- CSS Motion Path
- CSS Mask Effects
- CSS-Only Form Validation
- Scroll-Driven Animations
- Native Popovers
- Customized Selects

- Anchor Positioning
- Native CSS Carousels
- And more to come...

This book is for people who build interfaces and want to rely less on JavaScript when they do not have to. It is aimed at front-end developers, designers who code, and curious CSS people who already know the basics and want to see how far modern HTML and CSS can really go. If you have ever added JavaScript out of habit for something the browser can already handle, this book will give you a different way to think about that.

What will you learn

- Apply the Rule of Least Power in real UI decisions
- Choose modern HTML and CSS over JS where it's sufficient
- Build lightweight, accessible interfaces in practice
- Use modern CSS features like `:has()`, view transitions, motion paths, masks, popovers, and anchor positioning
- Create UI patterns like dark mode, dialogs, accordions, smooth scrolling, custom selects, and carousels
- Implement progressive enhancement in real projects
- Improve performance by reducing unnecessary JS

Working through this book

This is a practical book built around examples, not theory alone. It starts with familiar interface patterns, then gradually moves into more advanced CSS and newer platform features. The thread running through all of it is simple: choose the least powerful tool that can do the job well. Along the way, the book keeps coming back to the real questions that matter in front-end work, like accessibility, performance, browser support, maintainability, and how to make good trade-offs.

Conventions used

There are a number of text conventions used throughout this book.

`CodeInText`: Indicates code words in text, database table names, folder names, filenames, file extensions, pathnames, dummy URLs, user input, and Twitter handles. For example: "Here the parent `.card` changes only when one of its children has the class `.active`."

A block of code is set as follows:

```
/* Targets .card only if it contains an .active element */
.card:has(.active) {
  border-color: green;
}
```

> **Note**
>
> Warnings or important notes appear like this.

> **Tip**
>
> Tips and tricks appear like this.

Get in touch

Have a question, found a typo, or want to suggest an improvement? I'd love to hear from you! Email me at `hey@theosoti.com`

Need help with your CSS or website project? I'm available for freelance work. Let's work together, just reach out!

Want to keep learning more about modern CSS and web design? Check out `theosoti.com` for articles, code examples, and updates.

Feedback from our readers is always welcome.

General feedback: If you have questions about any aspect of this book or have any general feedback, please email us at `customercare@packt.com` and mention the book's title in the subject of your message.

Errata: Although we have taken every care to ensure the accuracy of our content, mistakes do happen. If you have found a mistake in this book, we would be grateful if you reported this to us. Please visit `http://www.packt.com/submit-errata`, click **Submit Errata**, and fill in the form.

Piracy: If you come across any illegal copies of our works in any form on the internet, we would be grateful if you would provide us with the location address or website name. Please contact us at `copyright@packt.com` with a link to the material.

If you are interested in becoming an author: If there is a topic that you have expertise in and you are interested in either writing or contributing to a book, please visit `http://authors.packt.com/`.

Part 1

Everyday Features

Every website, no matter how simple, needs a handful of core building blocks. A smooth in-page navigation, a modal, an accordion, ... These are the patterns visitors expect to work out of the box. In this part we'll re-create those familiar features with modern HTML and CSS, keeping things accessible and lightweight. They're the everyday components you'll reach for again and again.

So let's jump right in!

This part contains the following chapters:

- *Chapter 1, Conditionally Styling with :has()*
- *Chapter 2, Dark Mode in CSS*
- *Chapter 3, Smooth Scrolling to Sections*
- *Chapter 4, Native Modals with <dialog>*
- *Chapter 5, Accordions with Pure CSS*
- *Chapter 6, Pure-CSS Automatic Slider*
- *Chapter 7, Auto-Numbered Headings*
- *Chapter 8, Other Use-Case of Counter*

1

Conditionally Styling with :has()

For a long time, CSS selectors only looked downward into the DOM. You could target children, descendants, or siblings, but you couldn't ask anything about a parent. That gap forced developers to use JavaScript for what felt like a styling problem.

The `:has()` pseudo-class finally closes that gap. Often nicknamed the "parent selector", it lets you apply styles to an element based on what it contains. With `:has()`, CSS can now look both ways: not just down at descendants, but up and sideways into context.

Understanding :has()

At its simplest, `:has()` matches an element when something inside it meets a condition. In practice, that usually means checking whether it contains a certain descendant. The syntax is intuitive:

```
/* Targets .card only if it contains an .active element */
.card:has(.active) {
  border-color: green;
}
```

Here the parent `.card` changes only when one of its children has the class `.active`.

Think of `:has()` as a conditional filter: "apply this rule, but only if..."

Practical Use Cases

Let's examine real-world scenarios where `:has()` simplifies conditional styling therefore eliminating unnecessary JavaScript.

Styling based on form input

Highlight a fieldset when one of its checkboxes is checked.

Figure 1.1 - Final result: change color of fieldset when input is checked.

```
<form>
  <fieldset>
    <legend>Select Extras</legend>
    <label><input type="checkbox"> Extra Cheese</label>
  </fieldset>
</form>
```

With `:has()`, the CSS is as direct as the requirement:

```
fieldset:has(input[type="checkbox"]:checked) {
  border-color: green;
}
```

No JavaScript, no extra classes. The parent reacts instantly to its child.

Here's a Codepen to see the demo: `https://codepen.io/theosoti/pen/pvjgjBB`.

Conditional Styles for Navigation

Navigation menus often need to signal when a list item has a submenu. With `:has()`, you can check if a <li> contains a nested <ul> and style its link accordingly:

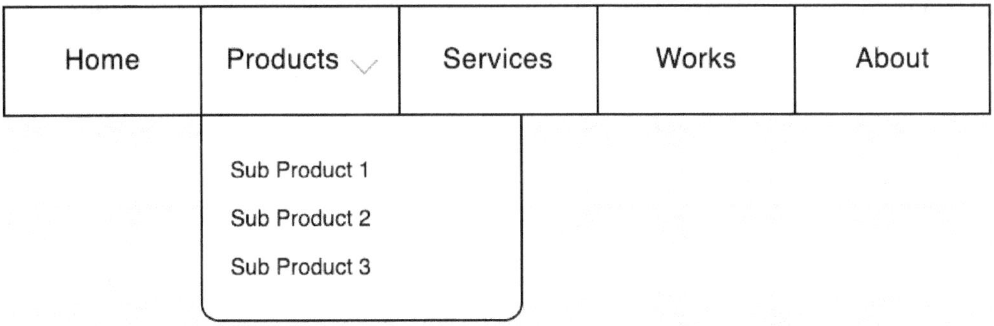

Figure 1.2 - Final result: arrow showing when the header has a submenu.

```
/* Show the arrow only if <li> has <ul> */
.nav-list > li:has(ul) > a::after {
  content: ">";
  transform: rotate(45deg);
}
```

The arrow appears only where it makes sense, without any manual markup.

Here's a Codepen to see the demo: `https://codepen.io/theosoti/pen/JoYGGdE`.

Advanced Combinations

`:has()` doesn't live in isolation. You can combine it with pseudo-classes to create rich conditional effects.

Here's an "inverted hover" pattern: when one card is hovered, all the others blur.

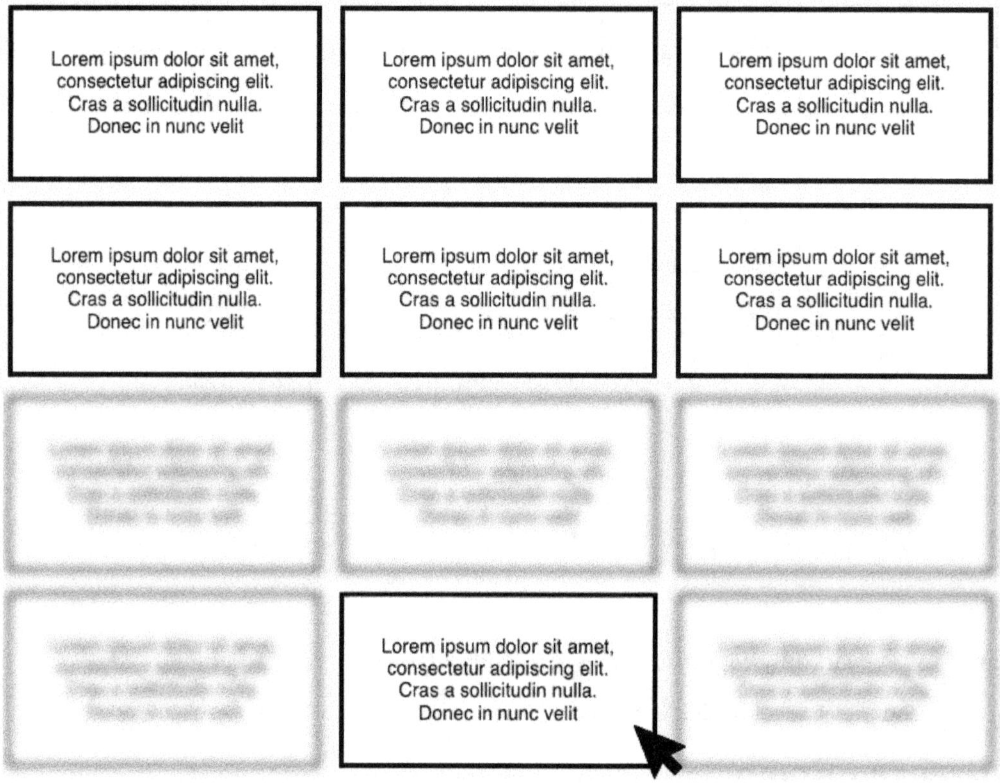

Figure 1.3 - Final result: hover an element blurs everything else

```
.cardlist:has(.card:hover) .card:not(:hover) {
  filter: blur(4px);
}
```

The parent `.cardlist` is what enables the effect. The `:has(.card:hover)` part checks if at least one card inside is being hovered. Once that condition is true, the selector matches the whole `.cardlist`.

From there, the `.card:not(:hover)` part comes into play. It says: "inside this card list, select all the cards that are not hovered." Those are the elements that get blurred.

The result is that the hovered card stays sharp, while every other card in the list gets blurred.

Here's a Codepen to see the demo: `https://codepen.io/theosoti/pen/VwJryJK`.

Checking adjacent siblings

Because :has() can look sideways as well as down, you can style an element based on what comes after it. For example, only apply a style to <h2> elements that are immediately followed by a paragraph:

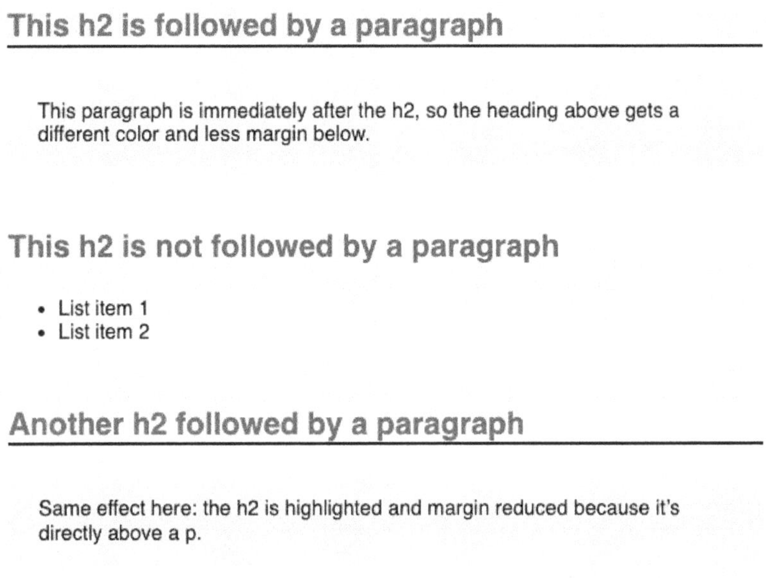

Figure 1.4 - Final result: second title is different because it has no paragraph.

```
h2:has(+ p) {
  border-bottom: 2px solid black;
  color: #555;
}
```

This lets you keep your headings context-aware without littering the HTML with extra classes.

Here's a Codepen to see the demo: https://codepen.io/theosoti/pen/ogjbbvW.

Changing layouts with a toggle

Perhaps the most dramatic effect is flipping layouts entirely with a single state. Imagine a list of cards that should switch between a two-column grid and single-column list, controlled by a checkbox.

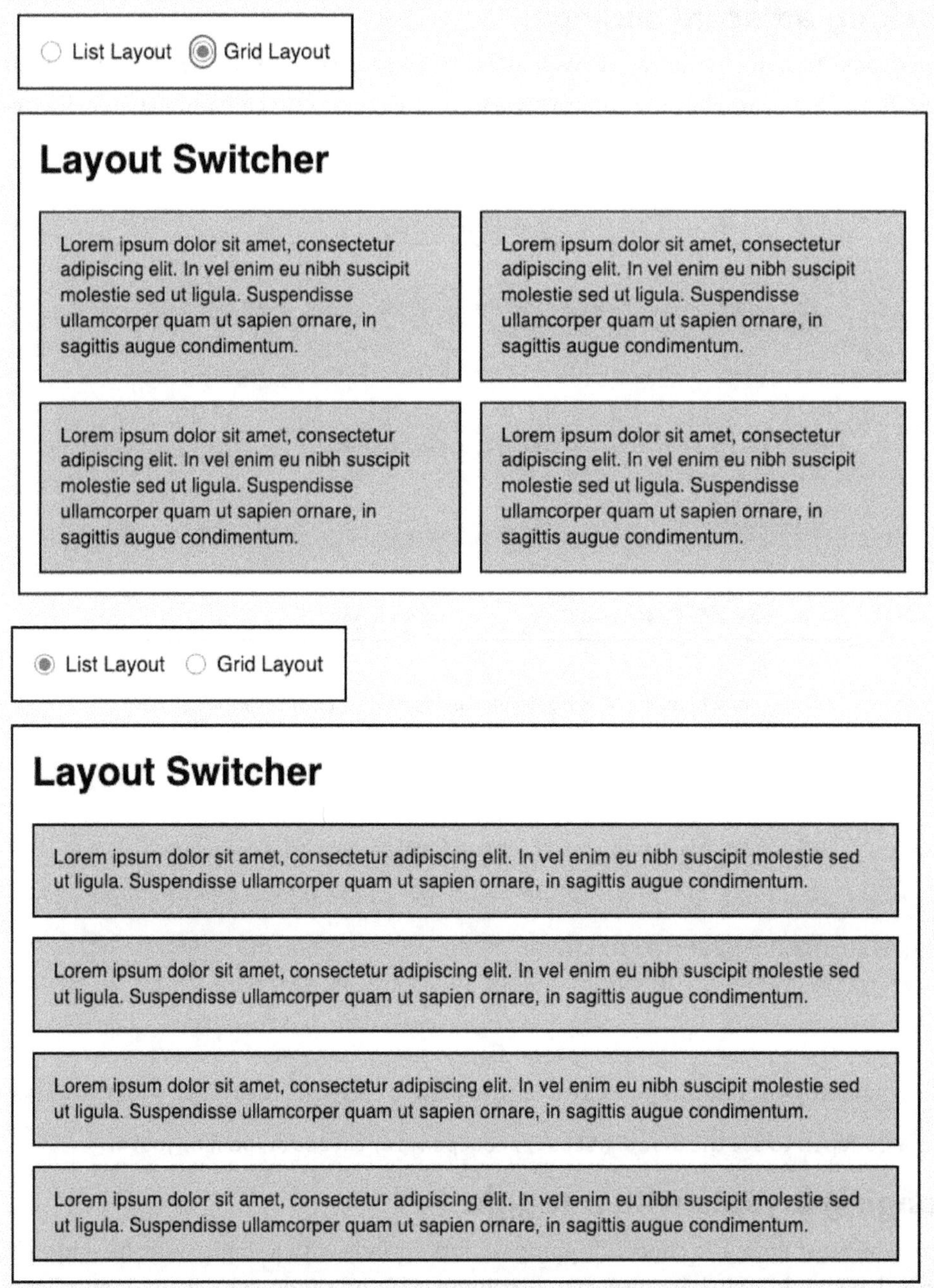

Figure 1.5 - Final result: Change the display of your content by checking a checkbox.

```
.card-list {
  display: grid;
  grid-template-columns: 1fr; /* default: single column */
  gap: 1em;
  padding: 0;
  margin: 0;
}

/* if the checkbox with "grid" id is checked, flip to two columns */
body:has(#grid:checked) .card-list {
  grid-template-columns: 1fr 1fr;
}
```

The trick is that `:has()` watches for the state of the checkbox. When it's checked, the `body` matches the rule, and the grid definition is swapped. Uncheck it, and the layout collapses back to one column.

Here's a Codepen to see the demo: `https://codepen.io/theosoti/pen/NWZjYPv`.

Browser Support and Fallbacks

Browser support (`https://caniuse.com/?search=%3Ahas()`) for `:has()` is already excellent (over 93.7% globally as of March 2026), but it's always smart to plan for the edge cases. That's where `@supports` comes in.

Think of `@supports` as CSS's built-in feature detection. Instead of trying to guess which browser is being used, you simply ask the browser: "Do you understand this feature?" If the answer is yes, the styles inside the block apply. If not, they're ignored.

Here's a simple example with `:has()`:

```
/* Fallback styling */
.feature {
  opacity: 0.5;
}
@supports selector(:has(*)) {
  .feature:has(.enabled) {
    opacity: 1;
```

```
    }
  }
```

In a modern browser, the `@supports` query succeeds and the enhanced rule kicks in. In an older browser, it fails gracefully, and the fallback style remains.

One last word on performance: `:has()` is powerful, but like any relational selector, it asks the browser to do extra work. A rule like `article:has(section ul li .active)` forces the browser to look several levels deep for every article, which can add up on large pages. Keeping your conditions simple (for example, `article:has(.active)`) is both faster and easier to maintain.

In short, use `@supports` to layer enhancements safely, and keep your `:has()` selectors focused. That way, you get the benefits of modern CSS without creating new bottlenecks.

Note

☑ **Key Takeaways**

- `:has()` dramatically reduces JavaScript reliance for conditional styling.
- Ideal for form interactions, navigation highlights, and state-based component styling.
- Enhances accessibility and UI responsiveness directly through CSS.
- Use carefully to maintain performance and compatibility

CSS is evolving, giving us tools like `:has()` that revolutionize how we build for the web. Embracing these features simplifies our work and creates more efficient, elegant experiences.

Next, let's see how to create a dark mode to adapt our designs seamlessly to user preferences and modern browsing environments.

2

Dark Mode in CSS

Modern operating systems let people choose between light and dark themes, and websites are now expected to adapt automatically. Supporting both modes isn't just about aesthetics, it improves readability in low-light conditions, reduces eye strain, and makes your site feel like it belongs on the platform.

The good news: you can build a robust dark mode with very little JavaScript.

In this chapter, we'll walk through each of the new CSS tools, step by step, and show how to combine them into a flexible dark mode system that respects both system defaults and user choices.

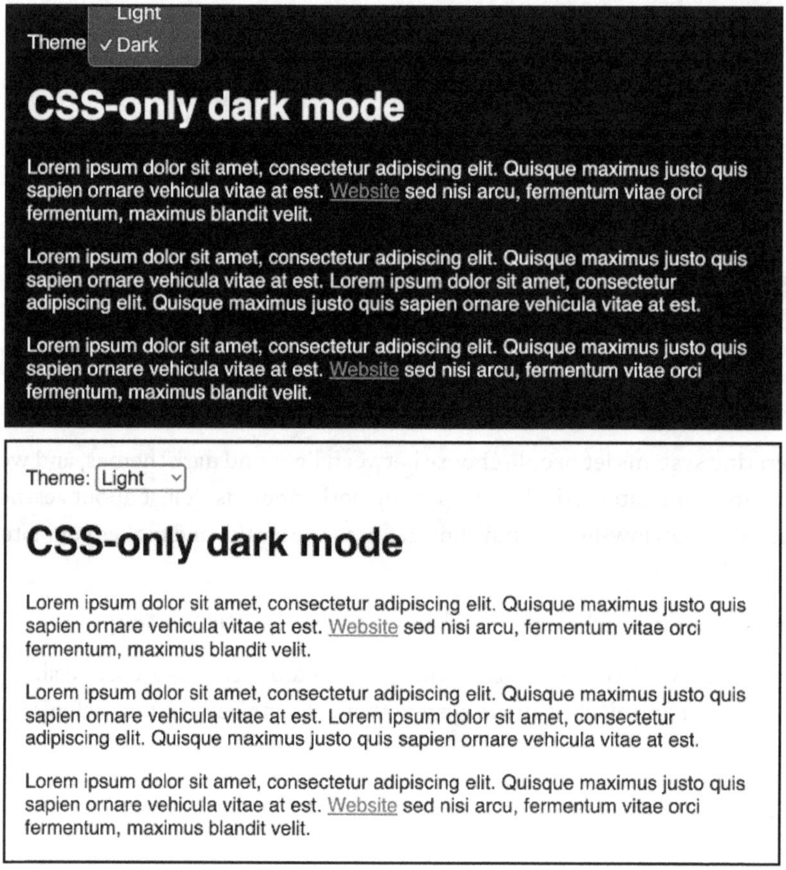

Figure 2.1 - Final result: Darkmode on the left. Lightmode on the right.

Detecting the System Preference

The first piece of the puzzle is detecting whether the operating system is set to light or dark mode. CSS gives us a built-in media feature for this: `prefers-color-scheme`.

```
@media (prefers-color-scheme: dark) {
  :root {
    --text-color: white;
    --link-color: deeppink;
    --background-color: black;
  }
}
```

```
@media (prefers-color-scheme: light) {
  :root {
    --text-color: black;
    --link-color: green;
    --background-color: white;
  }
}
```

Here's what's happening:

- `:root` is a special selector that matches the top-level element of the document (the `<html>` element in HTML pages). It's often used as a central place to define CSS variables.
- CSS variables (technically called custom properties) are the `--text-color`, `--link-color`, and `--background-color` you see above. Unlike ordinary CSS properties, these act like reusable variables: you define them once and reference them anywhere with `var(--name)`.

So in this example, when the OS is in dark mode, the first block runs and sets the variables to light-on-dark colors. When it's in light mode, the second block runs and sets dark-on-light values.

This means that as soon as someone visits your site, the browser applies the right theme automatically.

The light-dark() Helper Function

Writing both light and dark theme values separately can get repetitive. A new CSS function, `light-dark()`, helps streamline this.

```
:root {
  color-scheme: light dark;
  /* light-dark(lightValue, darkValue) picks the correct one */
  --text-color: light-dark(black, white);
  --link-color: light-dark(green, deeppink);
```

```
  --background-color: light-dark(white, black);
}
```

- The `color-scheme` property tells the browser your page supports both light and dark themes.
- The `light-dark(lightValue, darkValue)` function picks the right value automatically based on the current scheme.

So if the scheme is dark, `light-dark(black, white)` resolves to `white`.

> **Note**
>
> The `light-dark()` function is an emerging feature and not yet widely supported in all browsers. I will use it in this example for simplicity, but for maximum compatibility, you should still rely on `prefers-color-scheme` media queries mentioned previously.

Adding a User Toggle

System detection is great, but some users want manual control. For that, we can build a small theme switcher.

Figure 2.2 – Theme switcher

Here's a simple toggle using a <select> element:

```
<label for="theme-select">Theme:</label>
<select id="theme-select" name="color-scheme">
  <option value="system">System</option>
  <option value="light">Light</option>
  <option value="dark">Dark</option>
</select>
```

Now, with the power of `:has()`, we can conditionally set the `color-scheme` on `:root` depending on which option is checked:

```
:root {
  --text-color: light-dark(black, white);
  --link-color: light-dark(green, deeppink);
```

```
  --background-color: light-dark(white, black);
}

/* If the <select> element's value attribute matches, switch schemes */
:root:has(option[value="system"]:checked) {
  color-scheme: light dark;
}

:root:has(option[value="light"]:checked) {
  color-scheme: light;
}

:root:has(option[value="dark"]:checked) {
  color-scheme: dark;
}

body {
  color: var(--text-color);
  background-color: var(--background-color);
}

a {
  color: var(--link-color);
}
```

Users can pick their preferred theme from the dropdown, and the page will update instantly once you apply the selected value to the html element's `color-scheme` property.

Persisting User Choice with localStorage

> **Note**
>
> We're bending our "no JS" rule here with a tiny script. But just a few lines to remember your choice is a small price for a flawless experience!

There's one last problem: CSS alone can't remember the user's choice when they reload the page. For persistence, we add a tiny bit of JavaScript.

```
document.addEventListener("DOMContentLoaded", function () {
    const select = document.getElementById("theme-select");

    // 1. Load the saved theme, or fall back to the system
       preference
    select.value = localStorage.getItem("darkmode") || "system";
    select.setAttribute("value", select.value);

    // 2. Persist changes and keep CSS toggles in sync
    select.onchange = () => {
      localStorage.setItem("darkmode", select.value);
      select.setAttribute("value", select.value);
    };
  });
```

What this does:

1. On page load, we check `localStorage` for a saved theme.
2. If found, we set the `<select>` to that value (or "System" if not).
3. Whenever the user changes the dropdown, we update both the `<select>` and `localStorage`.

This keeps the CSS `:has()` selectors working and ensures the theme is remembered across visits.

Here's a Codepen to see the demo: `https://codepen.io/theosoti/pen/bGPpvZg`.

Note

ⓘ **Browser Compatibility (as of March 2026)**

- `prefers-color-scheme`: Fully supported in all modern browsers with over 95.5% global support (`https://caniuse.com/?search=prefers-color-scheme`).
- `:has()`: Fully supported in all modern browsers with over 93.7% global support (`https://caniuse.com/?search=%3Ahas%28%29`).
- `light-dark()`: Not fully supported with around ~85% browser support (`https://caniuse.com/?search=light-dark()`). Better using `prefers-color-scheme` for now.

Note

☑ **Key Takeaways**

- Detect system preference with the `prefers-color-scheme` media feature to provide automatic theming on first visit.
- You can use the `light-dark()` function to write concise, inline theme variables. But beware of browser support.
- Leverage CSS variables together with the `:has()` selector on form controls to switch themes without extra script logic.
- Persist user choice in `localStorage` so that manual theme selections survive reloads and revisits.

Now that your website gracefully adapts to user theme preferences, let's enhance another fundamental interaction: navigation. Using CSS alone, you'll create smooth scrolling effects that drastically improve the user's browsing experience.

3

Smooth Scrolling to Sections

On long pages with multiple sections, anchor links (`<a href="#section-id">`) are essential for navigation. By default, clicking one jumps instantly to the target. This works, but the abrupt snap can feel jarring. You lose context of where you came from, and if your site has a fixed header, the heading you navigated to often ends up hidden underneath it.

Modern CSS solves this with native smooth scrolling and scroll offsets. With just a few properties, you can create smooth, accessible navigation without writing a single line of JavaScript.

Smooth scrolling

The `scroll-behavior` property tells the browser how to move the viewport when a scroll happens. Either instantly (`auto`) or smoothly (`smooth`).

```
html {
  scroll-behavior: smooth;
}
```

On the `html` element, this makes the whole page scroll smoothly whenever you navigate to an anchor (`#section-id`).

By default, browsers keep this behavior consistent and safe: if the property isn't supported, scrolling simply falls back to normal jumps, nothing breaks.

To ensure consistent behavior everywhere, you can handle it yourself:

```
@media (prefers-reduced-motion: reduce) {
  html {
    scroll-behavior: auto;
```

```
  }
}
```

Smooth scrolling in scrollable containers

`scroll-behavior` also works on elements with their own scrollbars. This is useful for things like sidebars, chat windows, or code panels.

```
.sidebar {
  overflow-y: auto;
  scroll-behavior: smooth;
}
```

With this in place:

- If JavaScript scrolls the container (`element.scrollTo()` or `element.scrollIntoView()`), the scroll will animate.
- If a user tabs through inputs or focusable items inside the container, the browser will scroll smoothly to reveal them.

So, setting `html { scroll-behavior: smooth; }` makes all in-page links scroll smoothly across the entire page. But you're not limited to the page itself. You can also enable smooth scrolling inside any scrollable element, like sidebars, chat windows, or code panels.

Handling fixed headers

If your site uses a fixed header, there's a common problem: the section title gets hidden behind the header when you scroll to it. CSS provides two ways to fix this, depending on how global or precise you want to be.

Option A - Global offset

```
html {
  scroll-behavior: smooth;
  scroll-padding-top: 80px; /* match your header's height */
}
```

This adds an invisible buffer above every scroll target. No matter which section you navigate to, it always leaves 80px of space at the top.

Option B - Per-element offset

```
section {
  scroll-margin-top: 80px; /* match your header's height */
}
```

Here, the offset applies only to the elements you choose (for example, specific headings or sections). That means:

- Sections you don't tag with `scroll-margin-top` won't get extra spacing.
- You can give different elements different offsets, depending on their layout.

This is handy when some sections require more (or less) space than others.

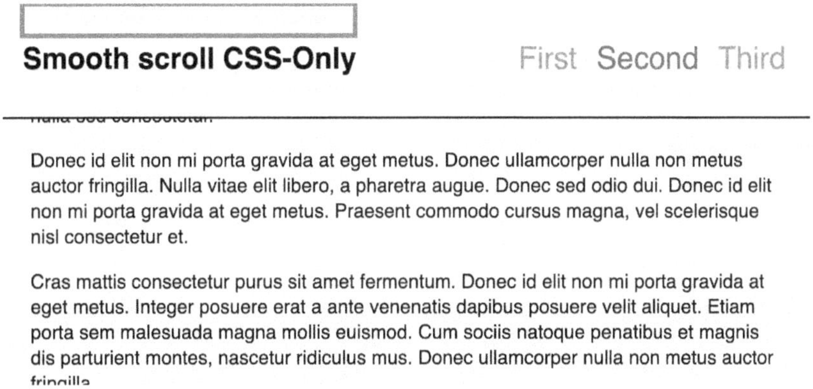

Figure 3.1 - Section title without offset.

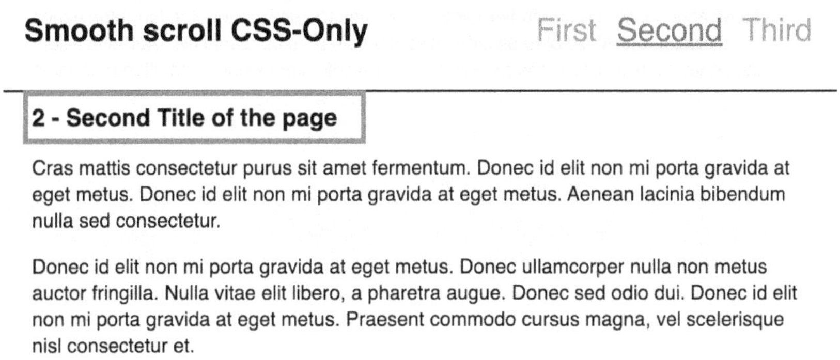

Figure 3.2 - Section title with offset.

Here's a Codepen to see the demo: `https://codepen.io/theosoti/pen/bGPpvZg`.

Note

ⓘ Browser Compatibility (as of March 2026)

- `scroll-behavior: smooth`: Fully supported in all modern browsers with over 95.6% global support (`https://caniuse.com/?search=scroll-behavior`).
- `scroll-padding-top` & `scroll-margin-top`: Fully supported in all modern browsers with over 95.9% global support (`https://caniuse.com/?search=scroll-padding-top`).
- Browsers who don't support it just won't display the animation.

Note

☑ Key Takeaways

- `scroll-behavior`: controls *how* scrolling happens, works on the page (`html`) or any scrollable container.
- `scroll-padding-top`: defines a global "safe space" above all scroll targets.
- `scroll-margin-top`: defines an offset on a per-element basis.
- Native CSS scrolling is fast to load, easy to maintain, and automatically respects accessibility.

With your page navigation now elegantly handled through CSS, let's move on to interactive UI components. You'll learn how the native HTML `<dialog>` element simplifies modals, delivering robust accessibility with minimal JavaScript.

4

Native Modals with <dialog>

Modals are everywhere: login forms, alerts, confirmation boxes. They let you display important information without leaving the current page. But for years, developers had to re-build them with a lot of JavaScript:

- Toggle visibility,
- Prevent interaction with the background,
- Trap keyboard focus inside the modal,
- Close it when pressing Escape.

That meant dozens of lines of code and a lot of accessibility edge cases.

The `<dialog>` element changes that. It's a native HTML element designed for dialogs, with built-in support for focus, background blocking, and accessibility. With a little CSS and one line of JavaScript, you get a modal that feels professional and reliable.

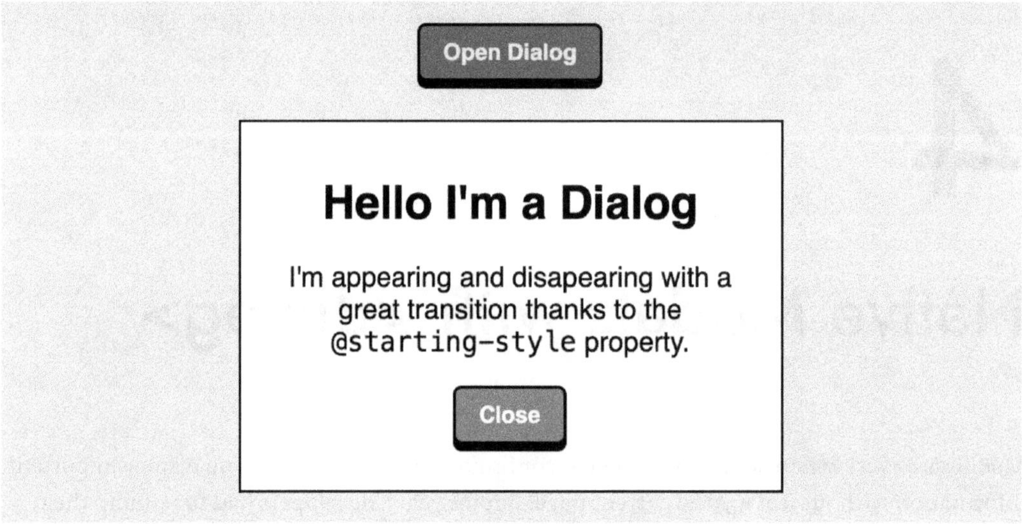

Figure 4.1 - Final result: dialog opened.

The Basic HTML Structure

A dialog is just another element in your markup. To open it, you need a regular interactive element (most often a button) that you'll connect with a tiny script.

```
<button id="open-dialog">Open Dialog</button>

<dialog id="modal" aria-labelledby="modal-title">
  <h2 id="modal-title">Dialog Title</h2>
  <p>This is a native modal using the HTML `<dialog>` element.</p>

  <form method="dialog">
    <button>Close</button>
  </form>
</dialog>
```

A few important details here:

- `aria-labelledby="modal-title"` links the dialog to its heading for screen readers.

- Any button inside a `<form method="dialog">` will automatically close the dialog by calling `modal.close()`. No script needed.
- When the dialog is open, the browser will trap focus inside it and make the background inert by default.

Opening the Dialog with JavaScript

To open the dialog, all we need is a single script:

```
const modal  = document.getElementById('modal');
const button = document.getElementById('open-dialog');

button.addEventListener('click',()=> {
  modal.showModal();
});
```

Calling `showModal()` tells the browser to open the `<dialog>` in "modal mode". That means interaction with the rest of the page is automatically blocked, focus is kept inside the dialog, and pressing the *Esc* key will close it. There's also a second method, `show()`, which opens the dialog without blocking the background. More like a popover than a modal. For most use cases you'll want `showModal()`.

If you need to close the dialog programmatically, you can call `modal.close()`.

Animating the Dialog

By default, `<dialog>` just appears or disappears when opened and closed. To make it feel more polished, we can add a simple animation using CSS transitions. In this example, the dialog fades and slides into place when it opens:

```
dialog {
  opacity: 0;
  translate: 0 -25vh;

  transition: translate 0.6s ease, opacity 0.6s ease;
}

dialog[open] {
  translate: 0 0;
  opacity: 1;
```

```
  @starting-style {
    opacity: 0;
    translate: 0 -25vh;
  }
}
```

The `dialog` starts off slightly above its final position (`translate: 0 -25vh`) and is completely transparent. When it opens, the browser adds the open attribute. That triggers the `dialog[open]` rule, resetting the transform and opacity to bring it smoothly into view.

The `@starting-style` block is progressive enhancement: it defines what the dialog looked like before opening, so the transition animates from that state. Browsers that don't support `@starting-style` simply fall back to the regular transition, so nothing breaks.

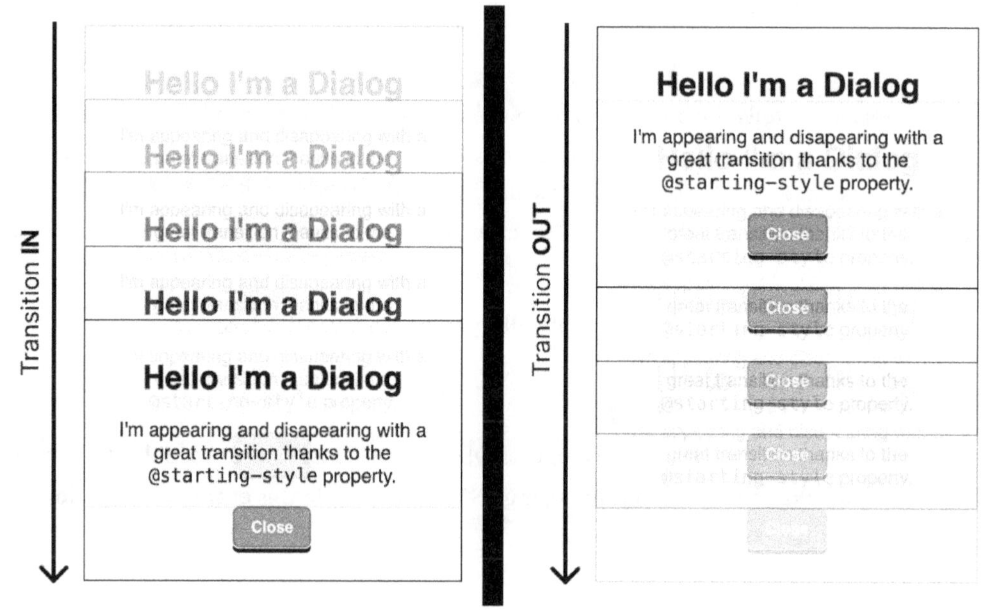

Figure 4.2 - The modal transition in and out.

Styling the Backdrop

Every dialog comes with a backdrop by default. It's a special pseudo-element, `::backdrop`, that covers the rest of the page while the modal is open. You can style it just like any other element:

```
dialog::backdrop {
  background: rgba(0, 0, 0, 0.6);
```

```
    backdrop-filter: blur(4px);
  }
```

Since the backdrop only exists when the dialog is open, these styles don't affect the page otherwise.

Here's a Codepen to see the demo: `https://codepen.io/theosoti/pen/WbvJXvZ`.

> Note
>
> ⓘ **Browser Compatibility (as of March 2026)**
>
> - `dialog` & `::backdrop`: Fully supported in all modern browsers with over 95.8% global support (`https://caniuse.com/?search=dialog`).
> - `@starting-style`: Not fully supported with around ~87% browser support (`https://caniuse.com/?search=%40starting-style`). Either do the animation in JS or use it as it is as progressive enhancement. Browsers who don't support it just won't display the animation.

> Note
>
> ☑ **Key Takeaways**
>
> - Using the HTML `<dialog>` element with `showModal()` requires minimal JavaScript.
> - CSS transitions on `translate` and `opacity` provide smooth entry animations.
> - The `dialog::backdrop` pseudo-element supplies a native overlay without extra markup.
> - `<dialog>` provides native focus trapping, Escape-to-close support, and correct ARIA semantics by default

Having streamlined modals with native browser capabilities, let's tackle another common UI pattern: accordions. Pure CSS accordions will help you organize content dynamically, enhancing readability without additional JavaScript.

5

Accordions with Pure CSS

Accordions are ideal for FAQs and optional content that you want to keep out of the main flow until needed. They present questions, definitions, or extra details in a tidy, collapsible format so readers can open only what interests them.

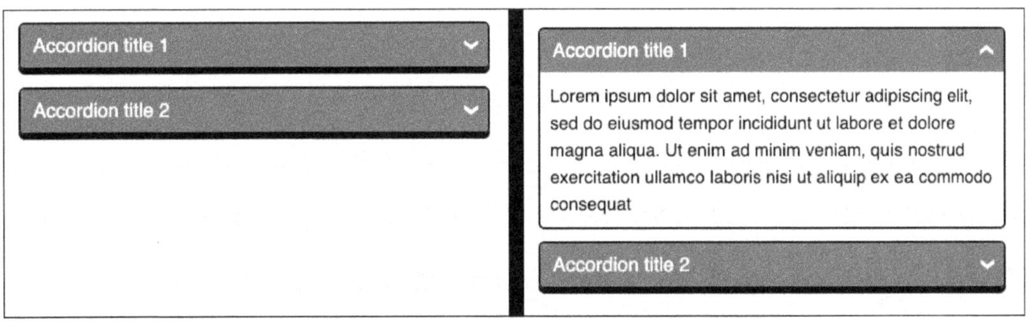

Figure 5.1 - Final result: Accordion closed on the left. Accordion opened on the right.

The Basic HTML Structure

We'll begin with semantic HTML. The core of our accordion uses the `<details>` and `<summary>` elements, an often-overlooked pair that gives us toggle behavior for free.

```
<details>
  <summary>
    <span>Accordion title</span>
  </summary>

  <p class="content">
    Lorem ipsum dolor sit amet, consectetur adipiscing elit...
```

```
  </p>
</details>
```

The <summary> acts as the clickable heading, and the paragraph contains the expandable content. This native structure keeps behavior predictable and accessibility-friendly.

Linking Multiple Accordions with name

If you give multiple <details> elements the same name value, the browser links them into one accordion group. In that group, only one item can stay open at a time, so opening one automatically closes the previously opened one.

```
<details name="faq">
  <summary>Accordion title 1</summary>
  <p>Lorem ipsum dolor sit amet...</p>
</details>

<details name="faq">
  <summary>Accordion title 2</summary>
  <p>Lorem ipsum dolor sit amet...</p>
</details>
```

This gives you classic "one-open-panel" accordion behavior with no JavaScript.

Showing Content by Default with open

You can add the open attribute directly in HTML to make an item visible on page load. This is useful when you want to highlight a default answer or keep important content immediately visible.

```
<details open>
  <summary>Accordion title 1</summary>
  <p>Lorem ipsum dolor sit amet...</p>
</details>
```

The open attribute controls only the initial state, and users can still expand or collapse items normally.

Built-In Find-in-Page Support (Ctrl + F / Cmd + F)

Another accessibility benefit is that find-in-page still works with accordion content. When users search with *Ctrl + F* on Windows/Linux or *Cmd + F* on macOS, matching text inside collapsed accordion panels can still be found, and supporting browsers reveal the matching panel automatically. This helps users locate information quickly, even when content starts in a collapsed state.

Hiding the Default Triangle

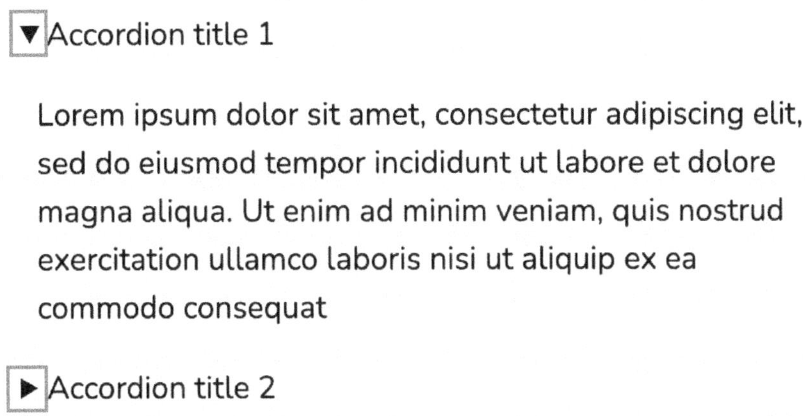

Figure 5.2 - Default browser arrows.

Browsers add a default triangle (called a disclosure marker) to `<summary>`. We remove it so we can use our own custom arrow:

```
summary {
  display: block;
}

summary::-webkit-details-marker {
  display: none;
}
```

Setting `display: block` ensures consistent layout across browsers. The second rule removes the built-in triangle in WebKit browsers like Safari and Chrome. Firefox hides it automatically once we apply custom layout styles.

Custom Arrow with :after

We'll now add our own arrow at the end of the summary using the `::after` pseudo-element:

```
span {
  display: flex;
  justify-content: space-between;
}

span:after {
  content: "\276F";
  transform: rotate(90deg);
  transition: transform 0.3s ease;
}
```

This uses a Unicode arrow (›) rotated 90 degrees so it points down. We space the arrow from the title using Flexbox.

To animate the arrow when the accordion opens, we update its rotation like this:

```
details[open] span:after {
  transform: rotate(270deg);
}
```

This gives the arrow a flipped effect to show the expanded state.

Smooth Content Animation

To animate the opening and closing while keeping native semantics, we style the built-in collapsible area directly, but first, let's specify something new:

```
:root {
  interpolate-size: allow-keywords;
}
```

Here, `:root` targets the top-level document element, so the setting applies globally. The declaration `interpolate-size: allow-keywords` tells the browser that transitions between numeric sizes and keyword sizes are allowed, which is important because we want to animate from 0 to auto.

Now we can style the built-in collapsible area:

```
details::details-content {
  block-size: 0;
  transition: block-size 0.3s ease, content-visibility 0.3s ease;
  transition-behavior: allow-discrete;
}
```

The pseudo-element `::details-content` targets the expandable content area inside `<details>`, meaning everything except the `<summary>`.

Setting `block-size: 0` keeps that content collapsed initially, since `block-size` is the logical equivalent of `height`. The transition declaration then defines how the expansion and collapse should animate, while `transition-behavior: allow-discrete` helps the browser handle properties like `content-visibility` in a smoother way instead of switching instantly.

As soon as the `<details>` element gets its native open attribute, the content area switches from `block-size: 0` to `block-size: auto`, so it grows to its natural height.

```
details[open]::details-content {
  block-size: auto;
}
```

With just that, you have a fully functional and animated accordion.

Now the last thing we can do is respect accessibility preferences:

```
@media (prefers-reduced-motion: reduce) {
  details::details-content,
  details span:after {
    transition: none;
  }
}
```

If a user has enabled reduced motion in their system settings, the transitions are disabled. The accordion still opens and closes correctly, but without animated movement.

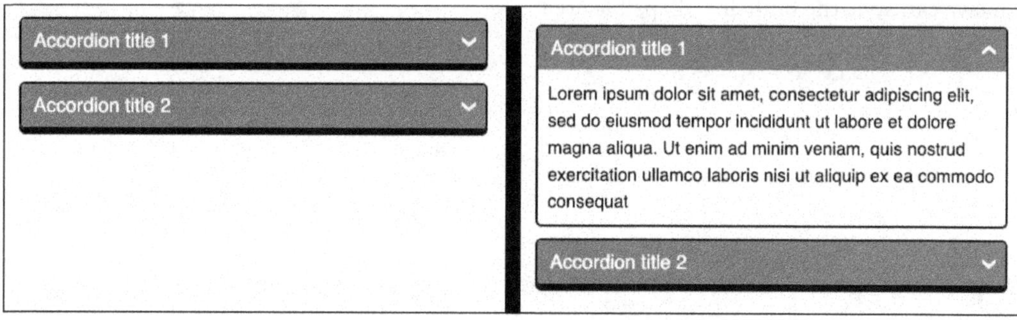

Figure 5.3 - Example of a finished accordion.

Complementary Native Features

Now that the accordion is fully built, there are three native behaviors worth knowing.

If you add the same name value to multiple `<details>` elements, they become a linked group. In that case, only one panel stays open at a time, and opening a new one closes the previous one automatically.

```
<details name="faq">
  <summary>Accordion title 1</summary>
  <p>Lorem ipsum dolor sit amet...</p>
</details>

<details name="faq">
  <summary>Accordion title 2</summary>
  <p>Lorem ipsum dolor sit amet...</p>
</details>
```

You can also use the open attribute to make an accordion visible by default when the page loads.

```
<details open>
  <summary>Accordion title 1</summary>
  <p>Lorem ipsum dolor sit amet...</p>
</details>
```

Finally, accordion content stays searchable with find-in-page. When users press *Ctrl + F* (or *Cmd + F* on macOS), matching text inside collapsed panels can still be found, and supporting browsers reveal the matching panel automatically.

Here's a Codepen to see the demo: `https://codepen.io/theosoti/pen/ZYWowMo`.

Note

ⓘ **Browser Compatibility (as of March 2026)**

- `details` & `summary`: Fully supported in all modern browsers. with over 93.3% global support (`https://caniuse.com/?search=details`).
- `transition-behavior: allow-discrete`: Not well supported with around ~86.7% browser support (`https://caniuse.com/mdn-css_properties_transition-behavior_allow-discrete`).
- `::details-content`: Not well supported with around ~82.7% browser support (`https://caniuse.com/?search=details-content`).
- `interpolate-size: allow-keywords`: Not well supported with around 70.5% browser support (`https://caniuse.com/mdn-css_properties_interpolate-size_allow-keywords`).

But, you can still use it as progressive enhancement. Browsers which don't support them will show instant open/close, no animation.

Note

☑ **Key Takeaways**

- `<details>` and `<summary>` create accessible accordions without JavaScript.
- Replace the default triangle using `::after` and CSS transforms.
- `::details-content` + `interpolate-size` enables smooth transitions where supported.
- Keyboard and screen reader support comes for free.
- Limited support is acceptable here because the fallback remains fully usable.

With interactive content neatly organized through accordions, let's now explore visual animation using CSS alone. We'll build a smooth, automatic slider, eliminating the need for bulky JavaScript libraries

6

Pure-CSS Automatic Slider

Partner-logo strips are everywhere — they signal trust and traction by showing who you work with. But look under the hood and most of them are bloated. A single-direction, no-controls marquee often ships with an entire slider library, runs jittery `setInterval` code that stutters on low-end devices, and leaves keyboard users unable to pause the motion.

With modern CSS, we can do better. Hardware-accelerated animations let us build a smooth, infinite carousel that needs no JavaScript at all. It's lean, responsive, and accessible.

Figure 6.1 - Final result: an infinite carousel moving from right to left.

The Basic HTML Structure

The markup is compact: a wrapper `<div>`, an unordered list of items, and a set of inline custom properties that configure the component.

```
<div class="slider"
     tabindex="0"
     aria-label="Logo carousel"
     style="--width:150px; --height:150px;
            --quantity:10; --duration: 10s;">

  <ul class="list">
    <li class="item" style="--position:1">
      <img src="img1.png" alt="img1"></li>
    <li class="item" style="--position:2">
      <img src="img2.png" alt="img2"></li>
    <!-- ...duplicate up to 10 -->
    <li class="item" style="--position:10">
      <img src="img10.png" alt="img10"></li>
  </ul>
</div>
```

Each inline property defines one part of the slider's logic:

- `--width` and `--height` → the size of each logo card.
- `--quantity` → how many items make up one cycle.
- `--duration` → how long a full loop takes.
- `--position` → the item's place in the sequence, so the animation knows when it should appear.

By using inline custom properties, the slider becomes self-contained and reusable. You can drop it anywhere on a page and configure its size, speed, or number of items without editing the CSS file.

The `tabindex="0"` makes the whole carousel focusable with the keyboard. That may not sound important yet, but we'll soon use it to let keyboard users pause the animation.

The Slider Container

The `.slider` acts as a viewing window. Its `overflow: hidden` ensures that only the visible part of the list is shown. To make the motion feel polished, we also add fading edges at the left and right, so logos glide in and out instead of popping.

```
.slider {
  width: 100%;
  height: var(--height);
  overflow: hidden;
  /* Fade-in/out at the edges so logos don't pop */
  mask-image: linear-gradient(to right,
                transparent,
                #000 10% 90%,
                transparent);
}
```

The `mask-image` creates a GPU-accelerated layer that fades out content near the edges. If the browser doesn't support masks, the slider still works — logos will just appear abruptly. A more widely supported fallback is to use pseudo-elements with gradients on `::before` and `::after`. That sacrifices a bit of performance but guarantees the same fading effect everywhere.

Inside the slider, the `.list` holds the items in a row:

```
.list {
  display: flex;
  min-width: calc(var(--width) * var(--quantity));
  position: relative;
}
```

Here `min-width` ensures there's enough room for all items, and `position: relative` sets up the coordinate system for absolutely positioned children, which we'll use in a moment.

Animating the Items

The key to the continuous loop is the `.item` animation. Each logo card has a fixed size, starts just off-screen to the right, and moves steadily to the left.

```
.item {
  /* 1. Dimensions */
```

```
  width: var(--width);
  height: var(--height);

  /* 2. Off-screen start */
  position: absolute;
  left: 100%;

  /* 3. Slide animation */
  animation: slide var(--duration) linear infinite;

  /* 4. Staggered delay */
  animation-delay: calc(
    (var(--duration) / var(--quantity)) * (var(--position) - 1)
    - var(--duration)
  );
}

/* 5. Animation */
@keyframes slide {
  from {
    left: 100%;
  }

  to   {
    left: calc(var(--width) * -1);
  }
}
```

Each item begins at `left: 100%`, just outside the right edge of the container. Over the course of `--duration`, it travels left until it has fully exited the view (`-1 × width`). Because the animation is linear and infinite, the motion is perfectly constant and loops forever.

The real trick lies in the `animation-delay`. Instead of starting all logos at once, we stagger them:

- A full loop lasts `--duration`.
- The gap between logos is `loop / quantity`.

- Each item's index (`--position`) sets how far behind it should be.
- Finally, subtracting one loop ensures the first frame already shows a full sequence in motion, so you never see an empty track.

```
loop            = var(--duration)
gap             = loop / var(--quantity)
index           = var(--position) - 1
animation-delay = gap × index - loop
```

Think of it like a relay race: each runner starts exactly when the previous one has advanced enough, so the baton never stops moving.

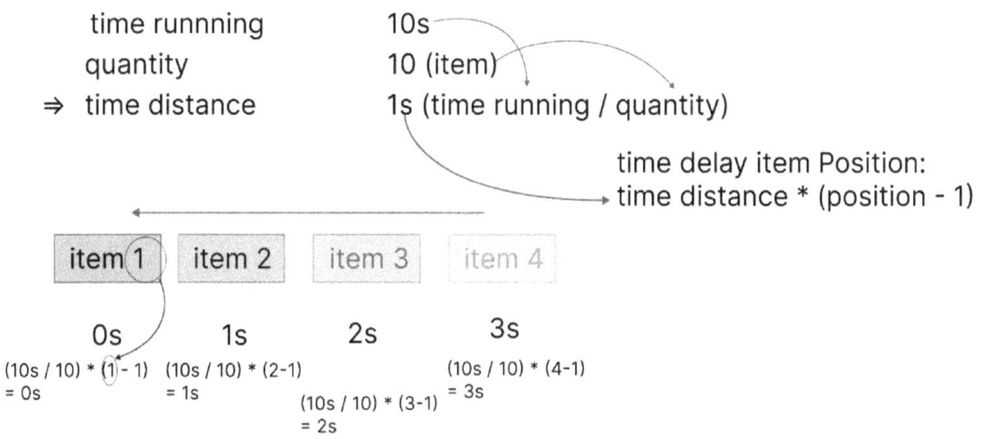

Figure 6.2 - Alternative explanation of the formula.

Pausing on Hover and Focus

An infinite motion can become distracting, so it's important to give users control. With just a few lines of CSS, we can let them pause it:

```
/* Hover with a mouse */
.slider:hover .item,
/* Focus with keyboard */
.slider:focus .item {
  animation-play-state: paused;
}
```

Hovering with a mouse stops the animation, and focusing with the keyboard (thanks to `tabindex="0"`) does the same.

Here's a Codepen to see the demo: `https://codepen.io/theosoti/pen/OPVeegy`.

> Note
>
> ⓘ **Browser Compatibility (as of March 2026)**
>
> - `mask-image`: well supported with 96.3% browser support (`https://caniuse.com/?search=mask-image`). But you can also use a simple fade-in/out gradient with `::before` and `::after`.
> - `animation-play-state`: Fully supported in all modern browsers. with over 96.7% global support (`https://caniuse.com/?search=animation-play-state`).
> - You can also respect the prefers-reduced-motion media query to turn off autoplay entirely for users who disable animations in their system settings.

> Note
>
> ☑ **Key Takeaways**
>
> - Inline custom properties make the slider copy-paste portable and editable by every user.
> - `@keyframes` + calculated `animation-delay` yield a seamless, gap-free loop without JS timers.
> - `mask-image` gives a professionally faded entrance/exit without repaint cost.
> - `:has()` delivers focus-pause accessibility previously only possible with JavaScript.

After mastering dynamic animations with pure CSS sliders, let's delve into another powerful feature often overlooked: CSS counters. You'll see how CSS alone can automatically number headings and animate numbers, simplifying content management and dynamic displays.

7

Auto-Numbered Headings

If you've ever written a long document, you know the pain of keeping section numbers in sync. Change the order of a chapter, insert a new subsection, and suddenly you're renumbering everything by hand.

CSS has a solution: counters. Think of them as a built-in page-numbering machine. Once set up, each heading labels itself automatically. You can shuffle, remove, or duplicate sections as much as you want, and the numbers always stay correct.

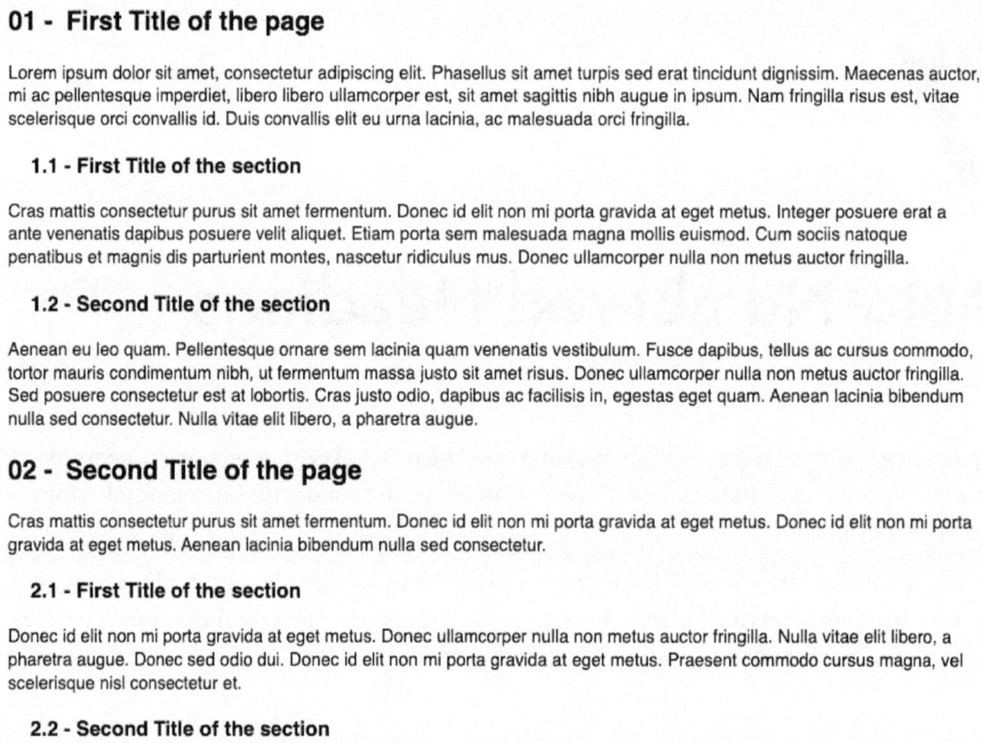

Figure 7.1 - Final result: Numbers in front of each heading.

Counters follow a simple rhythm:

1. **Reset** → start a counter at zero.
2. **Increment** → add one each time an element appears.
3. **Read** → display the current value with `content`.

That's all it takes. Let's walk through an example where `<h2>` elements become numbered section headings, and `<h3>` elements become numbered subsections.

The Basic HTML Structure

Here's a minimal structure with a couple of sections, each containing one or more sub-headings:

```
<main>
  <section>
    <h2>First title of the page</h2>
```

```
    <h3>First sub-title of the section</h3>
    <h3>Second sub-title of the section</h3>
  </section>
  <section>
    <h2>Second title of the page</h2>

    <h3>First sub-title of the section</h3>
    <h3>Second sub-title of the section</h3>
    <h3>Third sub-title of the section</h3>
  </section>
  ...
</main>
```

Numbering top-level headings

We begin by creating a counter called `h2`. Setting `counter-reset: h2` on the `<main>` element ensures the count starts fresh at the beginning of the document:

```
main {
  counter-reset: h2;
}
```

Each time the browser encounters an `<h2>`, it increments this counter:

```
h2 {
  counter-increment: h2; /* +1 for every h2 */
}
```

Now the counter exists and moves forward, but we don't see it yet. To display it, we use a `::before` pseudo-element:

```
h2::before {
  content: counter(h2, decimal-leading-zero) " - ";
}
```

The `decimal-leading-zero` style ensures numbers like `01, 02, 03`..., which helps line things up neatly.

At this point, every `<h2>` is automatically prefixed with its section number.

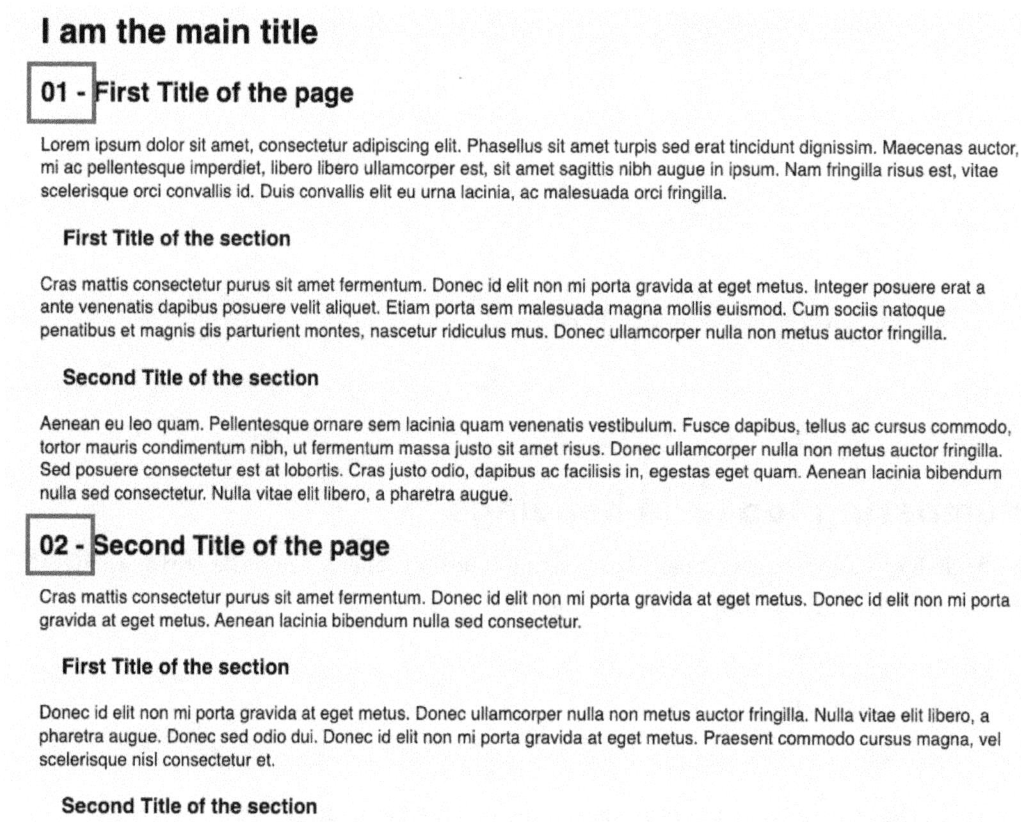

Figure 7.2 - Numbered h2 headings.

Numbering nested sub-headings

The real power comes when counters cascade. We can give each `<section>` its own local counter for `<h3>` elements. This way, every new section restarts its sub-heading numbers.

```
section {
  counter-reset: h3;
}

h3 {
  counter-increment: h3;
}

h3::before {
```

```
    content: counter(h2) '.' counter(h3) " - ";
  }
```

Here's how it works:

- Each `<section>` resets the `h3` counter to zero.
- Every `<h3>` increments it.
- The `::before` combines the current `h2` value with the current `h3` value.

So under `<h2>Second title of the page</h2>`, the first subsection becomes `2.1`, the second becomes `2.2`, and so on.

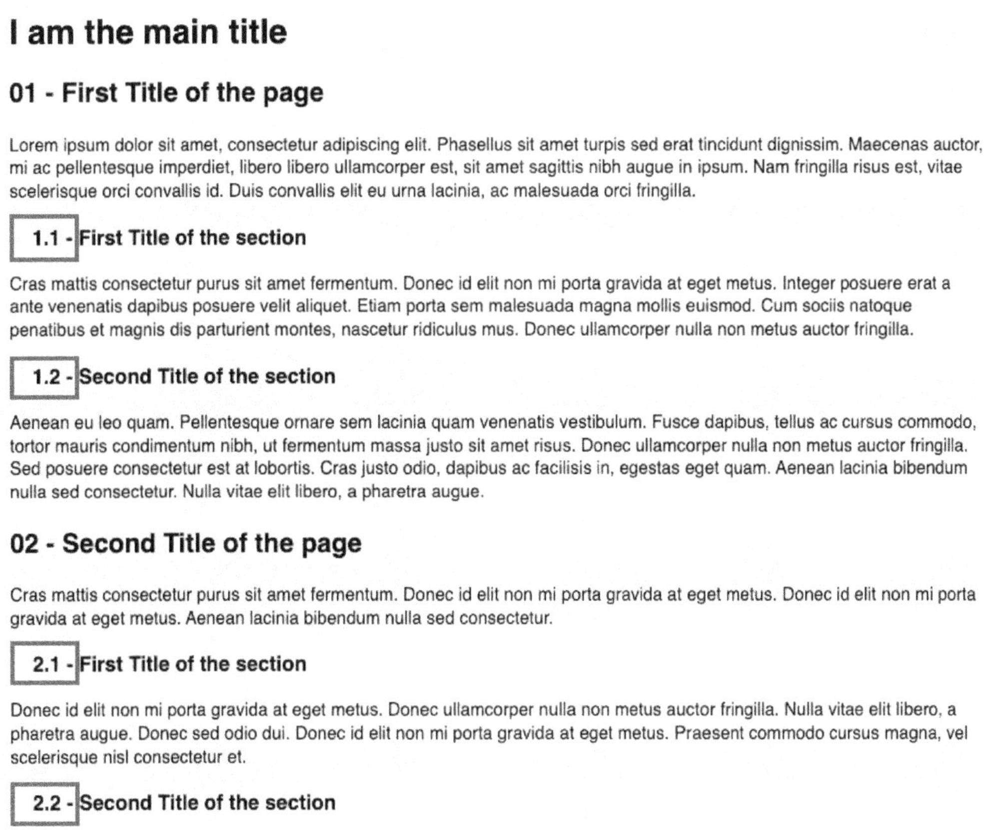

Figure 7.3 - Numbered h3 sub-headings.

Variations and styles

Counters aren't limited to plain decimals. The `counter()` function accepts a style parameter:

- `counter(h2, decimal-leading-zero)` → 01, 02, 03
- `counter(h2, upper-roman)` → I, II, III, IV
- `counter(h3, lower-alpha)` → a, b, c

You can even concatenate multiple counters to create multi-level numbering schemes. For example:

```
h3::before {
  content: counters(h2, ".") "-" counter(h3, lower-alpha);
}
```

This would yield something like `3-a`, `3-b`, and so on.

Here's a Codepen to see the demo: `https://codepen.io/theosoti/pen/YPXmEVg`.

We can now pivot from static labels to dynamic digits. Let's see how counters drive count-ups and index badges in the next part.

8

Other Use-Case of Counter

Numbering headings is the most common use of CSS counters, but they can do much more. Because counters are dynamic and can be tied to animations, they can label, inform, or even simulate behaviors we once thought required JavaScript.

One good example is an animated stat counter. The kind of effect you see in dashboards or landing pages, where a number rolls up from 0 to a target value. Traditionally this required JavaScript, but with modern CSS we can achieve it entirely in styles.

The effect we'll build here is a simple speedometer-like counter that climbs from `0` to `10`.

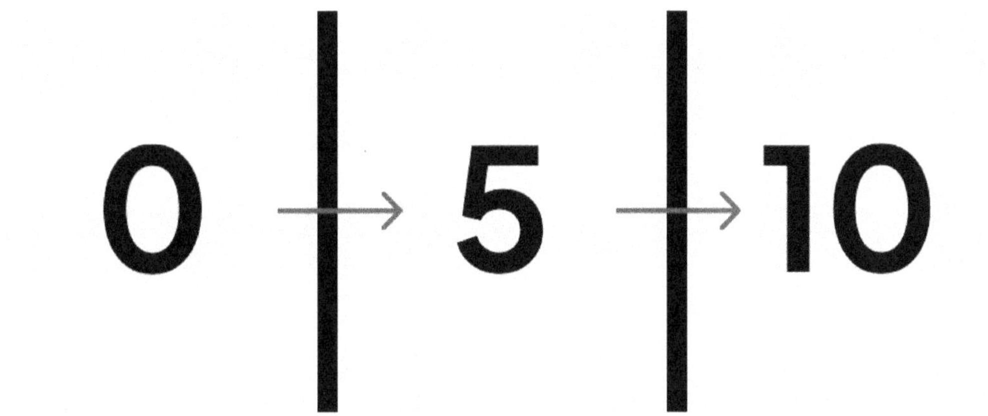

Figure 8.1 - Final result: counter from 0 to 10.

The Basic HTML

We only need a single element in the markup:

```
<div class="ticker" aria-label="10"></div>
```

Visually, this element will display the rolling number. But since the digits are generated with CSS, they aren't announced to assistive technologies. To fix that, we use `aria-label="10"`. That way, screen readers report the final value even if the animation itself is hidden from them.

Making a custom property animatable

To animate a number, we first need a custom property that accepts integers. CSS gives us the `@property` rule for exactly this:

```
/* Declare an animatable integer */
@property --c {
  syntax: "<integer>";
  initial-value: 10;
  inherits: true;
}
```

Here we define `--c` as an integer type. This makes it animatable, just like `opacity` or `transform`. Over time, we'll update `--c` from 0 up to the target value.

Driving the count with keyframes

Now we create an animation that modifies `--c` over time:

```
/* Timeline from 0 → target */
@keyframes countUp {
  from {
    --c: 0;
  }

  to {
    --c: 10;
  }
}
```

As the animation runs, the browser interpolates between the values and rewrites `--c` frame by frame. On its own, this doesn't produce visible text, we still need to display the number.

Print the counter

We can expose the changing value by copying `--c` into a real counter and then printing that counter with `content`:

```
/* Generate text from the running total */
.ticker::after {
  counter-reset: n var(--c);
  content: counter(n);
}
```

Here `counter-reset` takes the current `--c` value and stores it in a counter named `n`. The `content` property then prints that counter as text inside a `::after` pseudo-element.

Putting it all together

Now we tie the pieces together:

```
/* Kick off the animation */
.ticker {
  animation: countUp 5s linear forwards;
}

/* Big monospace digits, centred */
.ticker::after {
  font-size: 10rem;
  display: block;
  text-align: center;
}
```

The `.ticker` element runs the `countUp` animation once, taking five seconds to complete. Because we use `forwards`, the animation doesn't reset, it stops on the final frame, leaving the counter at 10.

The `::after` pseudo-element renders the digits in a large monospace font, centered on the screen.

Respecting reduced motion

Animations can be distracting or uncomfortable for some users. As always, we should respect their preferences by checking `prefers-reduced-motion`:

```
@media (prefers-reduced-motion: reduce) {
  .ticker {
    animation: none;
  }

  .ticker::after {
    content: "10"; /* jump straight to the value */
  }
}
```

This disables the animation for those users and simply shows the final value immediately.

Here's multiple Codepen to see what you can do:

- Heading counter (`https://codepen.io/theosoti/pen/YPXmEVg`)
- Counter up (`https://codepen.io/theosoti/pen/VYLwGwz`)
- Count the number of selected items (`https://codepen.io/theosoti/pen/RNNjrQe`)

> Note
>
> ⓘ **Browser Compatibility (as of March 2026)**
>
> - `@property`: Fully supported in all modern browsers. with over 94.5% global support (`https://caniuse.com/?search=%40property`).
> - Browsers who don't support it just won't display the animation.

> Note
>
> ☑ **Key Takeaways**
>
> - `@property` + `@keyframes` moves the value from 0 to the target.

- Display each frame by copying `--c` into a counter (`counter-reset`) and printing it with `content: counter(n)`.
- Expose `--target` and `--duration` so anyone can change the goal or speed with one line.
- Include the final number in markup (e.g., `aria-label="10"`) because pseudo-elements aren't read aloud.
- Wrap the animation in `@media (prefers-reduced-motion)` to show the static value when users prefer minimal motion.

You've now mastered handling everyday interactions and dynamic content using primarily HTML and CSS. But CSS doesn't stop there! Its latest capabilities can handle even more sophisticated UI patterns and interactions, pushing the boundaries of what's possible without JavaScript. In the next part, we'll explore these modern CSS power moves, introducing you to advanced components and creative techniques that will elevate your frontend skills even further.

Part 2

Modern CSS Power Moves

In this part we'll explore components and effects that are a little less common, but increasingly visible in modern interfaces: animated borders, mask effects, transition between pages, and more. These are the flourishes that give a site its personality. And we'll build them the same way as before: semantic, accessible, and almost entirely free of JavaScript.

This part contains the following chapters:

- *Chapter 9, Custom Border Animations*
- *Chapter 10, View Transitions*
- *Chapter 11, CSS Motion Path*
- *Chapter 12, CSS Mask Effects*
- *Chapter 13, CSS-Only Form Validation*

9

Custom Border Animations

Animated borders used to require heavy tricks: JavaScript continuously redrawing gradients, or SVG filters layered behind content. Today, modern CSS gives us all the ingredients natively. With a pseudo-element, a conic gradient, and the new `@property` rule, we can create glowing, rotating borders that feel alive.

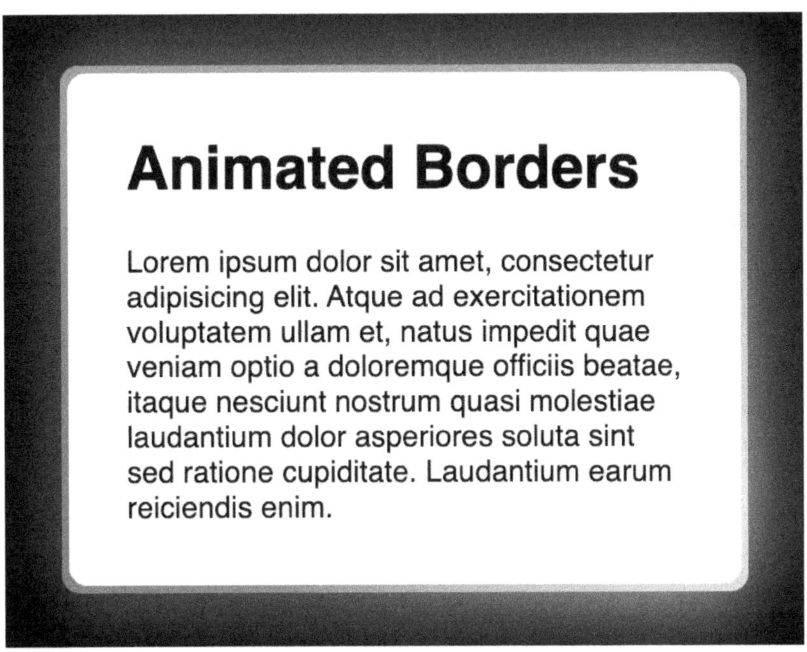

Figure 9.1 - Final result: glowing border moving indefinitely.

The Basic HTML Structure

The markup is minimal:

```
<div class="card">
  <!-- Your card content goes here -->
</div>
```

The work all happens in CSS.

Preparing the card

The card needs to establish itself as a positioning context so that its pseudo-elements can sit exactly behind it. It also needs a solid background to prevent the animated gradient from leaking through.

```
.card {
  position: relative;
  z-index: 1; /* keep content above the border */
  background-color: white; /* hides gradient behind the face */
}
```

Without the background color, the gradient layer we'll add would bleed through, competing with the card's content.

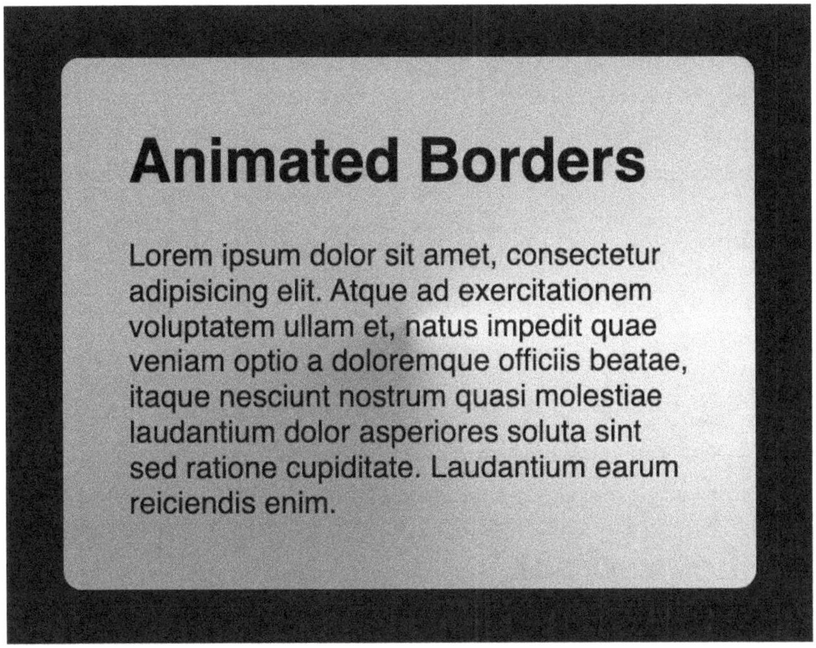

Figure 9.2 - Result if you don't add a background to the card.

Adding a border layer

We create the "border" not with `border` itself, but with a pseudo-element stretched slightly larger than the card.

```
.card::after {
  content: "";
  position: absolute;
  inset: -4px;  /* expand 4px beyond every edge */
  z-index: -1;  /* push it behind the card */
  border-radius: inherit;
}
```

The negative inset makes the pseudo-element stick out beyond the card, visually becoming its border. Inheriting the radius ensures corners line up perfectly.

Declaring an animatable property

We want this border to rotate smoothly. To do that, we need a custom property for the angle — but not all custom properties can animate by default. The `@property` at-rule tells the browser that `--angle` should behave like a real angle value, so it can be interpolated in keyframes.

```
@property --angle {
  syntax: "<angle>";
  initial-value: 0deg;
  inherits: false;
}
```

This registers `--angle` as an angle type, starting at `0deg`. The `inherits: false` ensures each card manages its own angle, rather than inheriting from a parent.

Drawing the gradient

Now we paint the border using a conic gradient that rotates based on `--angle`:

```
.card::after {
  /* ...previous declarations... */
  background: conic-gradient(
    from var(--angle),
    #ff4545,
    #00ff99,
    #006aff,
    #ff0095,
    #ff4545 /* repeat first stop for a seamless loop */
  );
}
```

The repeating first color stop avoids a visible jump where the gradient loops. Even without animation, this already produces a colorful border.

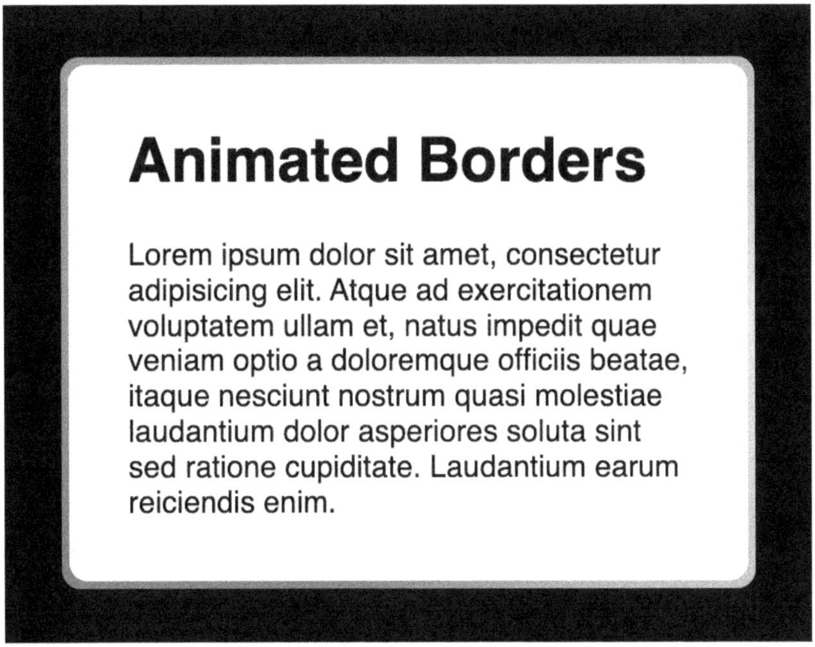

Figure 9.3 - Gradient border result (no glowing).

Animating the spin

To bring it to life, animate `--angle` from 0 to 360 degrees in an infinite loop:

```
.card::after {
  /* ...previous declarations... */
  animation: spin 3s linear infinite;
}

@keyframes spin {
  to {
    --angle: 360deg;
  }
}
```

The result is a smooth, endlessly rotating gradient border.

Adding the glow

The border already rotates, but we can make it feel more alive by giving it a soft halo. We do this by duplicating the gradient in another pseudo-element and applying blur.

```
/* Shared border setup for both layers */
.card::after,
.card::before {
  content: "";
  position: absolute;
  inset: -4px;
  z-index: -1;
  border-radius: inherit;
  background: conic-gradient(
    from var(--angle),
    #ff4545,
    #00ff99,
    #006aff,
    #ff0095,
    #ff4545
  );
  animation: spin 3s linear infinite;
}

/* Blur and fade the ::before layer for a glow effect */
.card::before {
  filter: blur(1.5rem);
  opacity: 0.8;
}
```

Here's what's happening in layers:

- The `::after` pseudo-element is our crisp, sharp border.
- The `::before` pseudo-element is the exact same gradient, but blurred and semi-transparent. The blur makes the bright colors spill outward beyond the edge, softening into a glow.
- Because both are positioned in the same place, the sharp version sits on top and the blurred version radiates beneath it.

Together, they produce the illusion of a glowing border without any extra graphics or images.

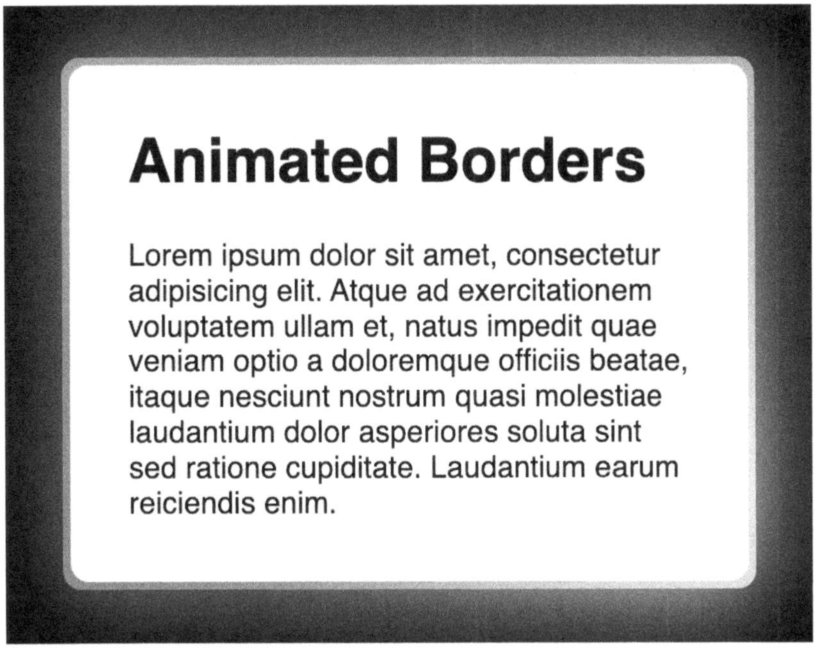

Figure 9.4 - Border + glow effect result.

Respecting reduced motion

Animations should never be forced on users who prefer static interfaces. We can turn the spin off gracefully with a media query:

```
@media (prefers-reduced-motion: reduce) {
  .card::after {
    animation: none;
  }
}
```

This leaves a colorful static border for users who opt out of motion.

Note

ⓘ **Browser Compatibility (as of March 2026)**

- `@property`: Fully supported in all modern browsers. with 94.5% global support (`https://caniuse.com/?search=%40property`). Non-supporting browsers show a static conic border.
- `conic-gradient`: Fully supported in all modern browsers. with over 95.6% global support (`https://caniuse.com/?search=conic-gradient`).

Note

☑ **Key Takeaways**

- Use a pseudo-element to draw borders without extra markup.
- Register `--angle` with `@property` so it can be animated.
- A conic-gradient combined with `from var(--angle)` produces a full-circle color effect.
- Animate `--angle` in keyframes for a seamless spin.
- Always include a `prefers-reduced-motion` fallback.

Border animations showed how even the smallest details can transform a component and make interfaces feel more polished. These flourishes demonstrate the creative power CSS has gained in recent years.

Now, let's see how entire page changes can be animated.

10

View Transitions

Page changes on the web have traditionally felt abrupt. Click a link, and the old page instantly disappears while the new one appears. That's fast, but it lacks the kind of smoothness we associate with native apps.

The View Transitions API changes that. It lets the browser capture a snapshot of your content *before* and *after* navigation, then animate between them automatically. Under the hood, the browser freezes the old content, layers the new one on top, and runs a transition. By default it cross-fades, but you can style it however you like: sliding, scaling, fading, or even more elaborate effects.

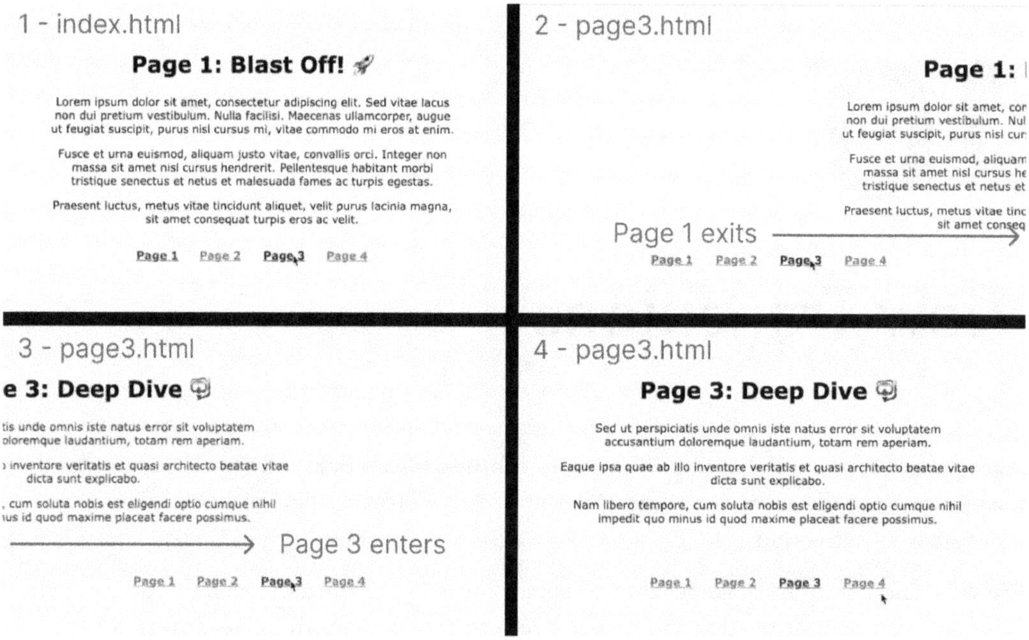

Figure 10.1 - Final result: pages transitioning by sliding from left to right.

HTML structure

You don't need any special markup, just consistency. Each page should have the same overall skeleton:

```
<main id="content">
  <!-- your page markup -->
  <h1>Page 1</h1>
  <p>Some content...</p>
</main>

<nav>
  <a href="index.html" class="active">Page 1</a>
  <a href="page2.html">Page 2</a>
  <a href="page3.html">Page 3</a>
  <a href="page4.html">Page 4</a>
</nav>
```

The `<main>` region will hold the part of the page that changes, while the `<nav>` stays consistent. Keeping this structure identical across pages helps the browser align transitions cleanly.

Opting into transitions

To activate view transitions across same-origin pages, add this global rule:

```
@view-transition {
  navigation: auto;
}
```

This tells the browser: "when navigating between documents, try to animate instead of instantly replacing." If either the current page or the destination page lacks this rule, the transition won't run. Browsers that don't support the feature simply fall back to normal navigation, so you lose nothing.

Choosing what animates

By default, the whole viewport fades. To take control, assign a transition name to the part of the page you want to animate:

```
#content {
  view-transition-name: content;
}
```

Here, the browser takes a snapshot of `#content` on both pages and links them together under the name `content`. Only elements with the same name across both pages are paired up for animation.

Styling the snapshots

The magic happens through two special pseudo-elements:

```
::view-transition-old(content) {
  animation: translate-out 400ms linear both;
}

::view-transition-new(content) {
```

```
  animation: translate-in 400ms linear both;
}
```

- `::view-transition-old(content)` targets the frozen snapshot of the element from the *previous* page.
- `::view-transition-new(content)` targets the snapshot of the element on the *next* page.

In this example, the old content slides out while the new content slides in. Remember, if you don't provide custom animations, the browser defaults to a cross-fade.

Defining the motion

The keyframes below create a simple left-to-right swap:

```
@keyframes translate-out {
  to {
    translate: 100vw 0;
  }
}

@keyframes translate-in {
  from {
    translate: -100vw 0;
  }
}
```

The old snapshot moves right off-screen, while the new one enters from the left. Because these animations run on snapshots, the actual layout of either page stays completely stable. Your DOM is updated instantly, the user only sees the transition layered above it.

I have no codepen to share because we can't navigate in it. But you can check an example here: `https://view-transitions.chrome.dev/pagination/spa/`

Respect reduced-motion

Always offer a fallback for users who prefer no animation.

```
@media (prefers-reduced-motion: reduce) {
  @view-transition {
    animation: none;
```

```
    }
}
```

Note

ⓘ **Browser Compatibility (as of March 2026)**

- `@view-transition`: ~82.5% global support (`https://caniuse.com/?search=%40view-transition`).
- `::view-transition-old()` & `::view-transition-new()`: ~90.7% global support (`https://caniuse.com/?search=view-transition-old()`).
- In unsupported browsers, it is simply ignored

Note

☑ **Key Takeaways**

- One at-rule and an attribute to animate view changes.
- Mark your element → enable transitions → style old → style new → define keyframes.
- Graceful fallback included.

Page-to-page transitions proved that CSS can now handle big, structural animations natively, without frameworks or plugins. This is a huge win for smoother, faster navigation.

Next up, we'll guide elements along custom paths.

11

CSS Motion Path

Motion Path is the name of the specification that introduces `offset-path`, `offset-distance`, and related properties. Together, these let you describe a shape (the path) and move an element along it, in pure CSS.

We'll keep this as small as possible: one container, one SVG path, one square. No extra styling, no helper wrappers.

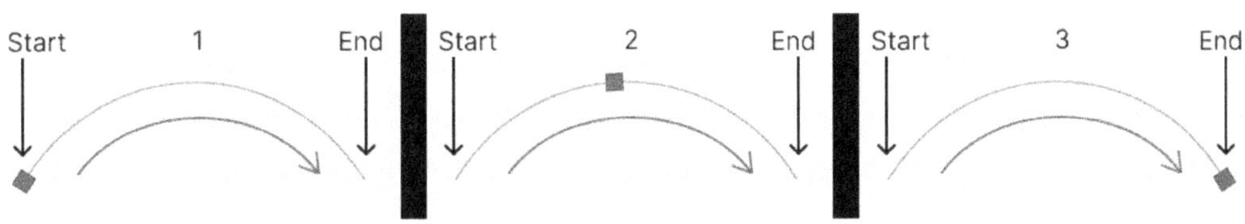

Figure 11.1 - Final result: going from left to right following the curve.

The Basic HTML Structure

We'll start by creating an SVG path for the element to follow. In this example we're using a curve, but the path could be any shape as long as it's defined in the SVG.

```
<div class="container">
  <svg viewBox="0 0 300 140" aria-hidden="true">
    <path d="M16,120 C80,20 220,20 284,120" />
  </svg>

  <div class="box"></div>
</div>
```

- <svg> is the "map" area, with a size of 300 x 140 units.
- <path> draws a curve (a C-shaped line) inside that map (you can use a tool like Easy Code Tools' SVG Path Builder (`https://easycodetools.com/tool/svg-path-builder`) to create your own path).
- `<div class="box">` is the square we'll animate later. In practice, this can be any element: an icon, an image, a button, or even a more complex component.

Figure 11.2 - The raw svg we drew.

Draw the route

At this point the path exists, but by default it shows up as a filled black shape (because SVG paths have a black fill unless you override it). Here we just need the curve to be visible as a line, like a track.

First, we make sure the SVG itself stretches exactly over the container:

```
svg {
  position: absolute;
  inset: 0;
  width: 100%;
  height: 100%
}
```

Then we style the path itself:

```
path {
  fill: none;
  stroke: #999;
  stroke-width: 2;
}
```

You should now see a thin gray curve across the container. This curve is the track for the motion path.

Figure 11.3 - Only the route displayed.

Make the Container Match the SVG dimensions

Here's a subtle but critical detail: the container (here `<div class="container">`) must match the SVG's dimensions. Why? Because the Motion Path positions the moving element relative to the container. If your SVG defines its drawing area with `viewBox="0 0 300 140"`, that means the path is drawn on a grid that is 300px wide and 140px tall.

To make the path and the moving element line up, the container should be set to the same size:

```
.container {
  position: relative;
  width: 300px;
  height: 140px;
}
```

If the sizes don't match, the square will still move, but it won't appear to follow the visible curve.

Draw the square

Let's create a square 14px wide. By default, the motion path positions the element's center on the curve, so the square will sit neatly on the path without extra alignment.

```
.box {
  position: absolute;
  top: 0;
  left: 0;
  width: 14px;
  height: 14px;
  background: #e6007a;
}
```

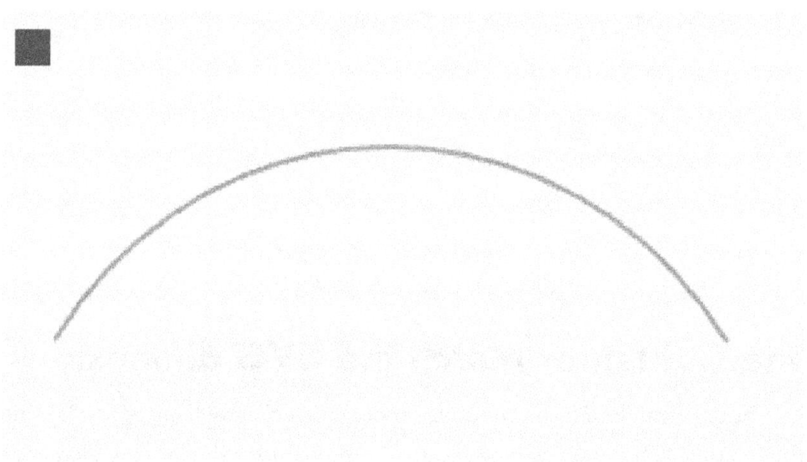

Figure 11.4 - The square is here, but we have to place it correctly.

Give it a path to follow

Paste the same `d` string from the SVG into `offset-path: path('...')`. Reusing the identical numbers keeps animation and drawing perfectly aligned. Also set `offset-distance: 0%;` so that the square starts at the beginning of the path.

```
.box {
  offset-path: path('M16,120 C80,20 220,20 284,120');
```

```
  offset-distance: 0%;
}
```

Figure 11.5 - Everything is now in place.

Animate along the curve

Drive the motion by animating `offset-distance` from `0%` to `100%`. The `alternate` direction sends the square back without further work. If you later replace the square with an arrow and want it to face the direction of travel, add `offset-rotate: auto`.

```
@keyframes move {
  to {
    offset-distance: 100%;
  }
}

.box {
  animation: move 3s ease-in-out infinite alternate;
}
```

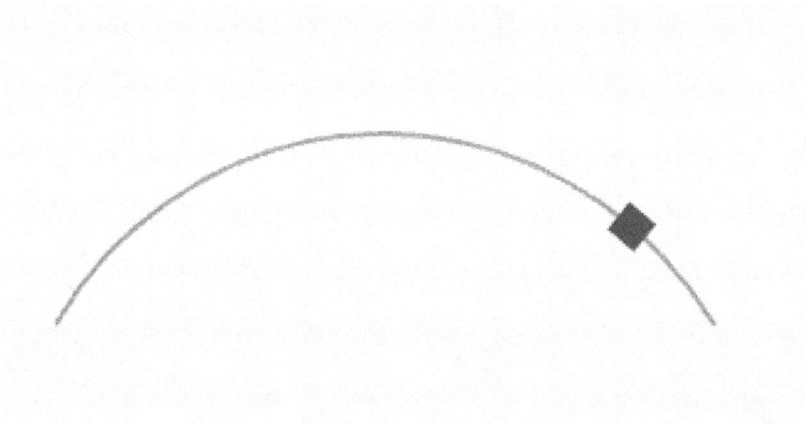

Figure 11.6 - The square is now moving.

Optional Path Visibility

The visible SVG line we drew is just a guide. It helps during development to see the curve your element is following, but it isn't required for the animation to work.

The only critical piece is the `d` string that you paste into `offset-path`. Once the animation is in place, you can safely remove the stroke, or even the `<svg>` entirely, if you don't need a visible trace.

For example, you can hide the outline simply by removing the `stroke` properties:

```
path {
  fill: none;
  /* stroke removed -- path is now invisible */
}
```

The square (or whatever element you animate) will still follow the curve perfectly.

Figure 11.7 - The square is moving without the visual line.

Use the outline when you want users to see a track, skip it when you want a "floating" effect.

Accessibility

Animations can be distracting or uncomfortable for some users. As always, we should respect their preferences by checking `prefers-reduced-motion`:

```
@media (prefers-reduced-motion: reduce) {
  .box {
    animation: none; /* stop the movement */
  }
}
```

In some cases, the moving element doesn't add any real value on its own. If it's purely decorative, it might be better to hide it entirely when motion is disabled:

```
@media (prefers-reduced-motion: reduce) {
  .box {
    display: none; /* remove it if animation isn't meaningful */
  }
}
```

That way you respect the user's preferences and keep the page free of distractions.

Troubleshooting

If the square travels near the line rather than on it, check these three things in order:

- Make sure the container's CSS width and height match the dimensions defined in the SVG's `viewBox` (300 × 140 in this example).
- Verify that the CSS `path('...')` string and the SVG `d="..."` value are character-for-character identical.
- Ensure the square starts at the origin with `top: 0; left: 0;`.

When you need the curve to resize fluidly with the layout, the simplest approach is to scale the entire stage. If the curve must actually reshape, you'll need to update the path data, which is one of the few cases where a tiny bit of JavaScript to generate coordinates can be justified.

Here's a Codepen to see the demo: `https://codepen.io/theosoti/pen/EaVvBwz`.

> Note
>
> ⓘ **Browser Compatibility (as of March 2026)**
>
> - `offset-path`, `offset-distance`, and `offset-rotate`: ~95.4% global support (`https://caniuse.com/?search=offset-distance`).
> - In older engines that ignore these properties, the square remains static while the rest of the page renders normally. Ship a non-animated fallback if your audience includes those browsers.

> Note
>
> ☑ **Key Takeaways**
>
> - Use `offset-path: path('...')` and animate `offset-distance` to move an element along any curve.
> - Keep the container size equal to the SVG `viewBox` and reuse the same `d` string in CSS for perfect alignment.
> - Start with a simple shape (a square or dot) so the center rides the path naturally. Add `offset-rotate` (and, if needed, `offset-anchor`) only for directional artwork.

- Honor `prefers-reduced-motion` to provide a no-animation experience.
- Treat responsiveness by scaling the whole component, regenerate path data only if the curve itself must reshape.

Motion Path gives you the ability to choreograph precise movement, bringing individuality and playfulness to your designs. It shows how CSS animation has matured beyond simple transforms.

Now, let's discover how masks can shape what's visible.

12

CSS Mask Effects

Masks let you control which parts of an element are visible using another image or gradient as a visibility map. Opaque areas of the mask reveal the element, while transparent areas hide it. Think of it as cutting a stencil and then shining your element through it.

In this chapter we'll use masks to build a practical before/after slider powered by a native <input type="range">. Then we'll explore two more use cases to show how flexible this technique can be.

Figure 12.1 - Final result: 2 sections that can show or hide by a percentage.

The Basic HTML Structure

Two sibling sections (`.before` and `.after`) sit in the same slot, plus a native range on top. This example uses text panels, but you can drop in images just the same.

```
<label for="compare-range">Compare</label>
```

```
<div class="compare" style="--pos: 50%">
  <section class="before">I'm the left section 😻</section>
  <section class="after">I'm the right section 🙀</section>

  <input
    type="range"
    id="compare-range"
    min="0" max="100" step="0.1" value="50"
    aria-label="Comparison position"
  />
</div>
```

The range stays native (keyboard/touch accessible) and provides a value you can read or submit. Here's the explanation:

- `min` / `max` → define the scale. We use `0–100` so the slider value maps directly to a percent for `--pos`.
- `step` → sets granularity (and keyboard increments). `0.1` is silky, `1` is whole percent.
- `value` → the starting position so the divider and `--pos` match on load.

The two panels are just regular elements that we'll reveal with masks.

Stacking everything with grid

We need the panels and slider to overlap perfectly. One option would be absolute positioning with `top: 0; left: 0; right: 0; bottom: 0;`. But that requires extra CSS and breaks easily when the container resizes.

Instead, we let CSS Grid do the work:

```
.compare {
  display: grid;
}

.compare > * {
  grid-area: 1 / 1;       /* stack sections + slider */
}

section {
  display: grid;
  align-items: center;
  justify-content: center;
```

```
    text-align: center;
}
```

Because every child shares the same grid cell, they naturally stack without math or offsets. Resize the container, and everything still lines up.

Figure 12.2 - Everything elements are now on top of each other.

Complementary masks

Now the panels need to split at the slider's position. That's where masks come in.

```
/* Left side: show from 0 → --pos, then hide */
.before {
  background: #fff8f0;
  -webkit-mask: linear-gradient(to right, #000 0, var(--pos), transparent 0);
  mask: linear-gradient(to right, #000 0, var(--pos), transparent 0);
}

/* Right side: hide from 0 → --pos, then show */
.after {
  background: #122b1f;
  color: #fff8f0;
  -webkit-mask: linear-gradient(to right, transparent 0, var(--pos), #000 0);
  mask: linear-gradient(to right, transparent 0, var(--pos), #000 0);
}
```

Let's break down the left panel (`.before`):

- At 0%, the gradient is black (`#000`), which means "fully visible."

- It stays black until the slider position (`--pos`).
- Immediately after `--pos`, it switches to transparent, which hides the rest.

The right panel does the opposite: it stays hidden until `--pos`, then switches to black.

The result is two complementary halves that meet exactly at the slider's position. Together, they form a seamless cut.

> Note
>
> 💡 **Safari/WebKit tip**:
>
> For broader coverage, duplicate each `mask:` as `-webkit-mask:` with the same gradient.

Figure 12.3 - The sections are now split in half.

Styling the slider

The range input needs to look like a clean divider rather than a native control. First, we strip away the default styles and hide the track:

```
.compare input[type="range"] {
  z-index: 1;
  appearance: none;
  background: transparent;
}
```

At this point, the slider is still functional, but invisible. Next we redefine its thumb (the draggable part) so it becomes a vertical bar:

```
/* The thumb becomes the vertical divider */
.compare input[type="range"]::-webkit-slider-thumb {
  appearance: none;
  inline-size: 4px;
  block-size: 100%;
```

```
  background: #000;
}

.compare input[type="range"]::-moz-range-thumb {
  appearance: none;
  inline-size: 4px;
  block-size: 100%;
  background: #000;
}
```

With these rules, the thumb itself *is* the divider. Dragging it will updates the mask position, so visually it feels like you're pulling the line that separates the two panels.

> **Note**
>
> ⓘ Browsers use different `range-thumb` pseudo-elements. If you group them in one rule, each browser sees an unknown selector and drops the entire rule. Write two separate rules so each engine applies the one it recognizes.

Updating the divider with JavaScript

The range input updates the `--pos` variable, which both masks use as their cut point. A small script handles this:

```
const range = document.getElementById("compare-range");
range.oninput = () =>
  document.body.style.setProperty("--pos", range.value + "%");
```

Each time the slider moves, `--pos` changes, and the masks redraw instantly so the divider follows.

Link to the codepen: `https://codepen.io/theosoti/pen/JojrrgB`.

Accessibility

Since the slider is a standard `<input type="range">`, it already works with:

- Mouse and touch
- Keyboard (arrows, PageUp/Down, Home/End)
- Assistive technologies

Provide a visible label or an `aria-label` to name the control. Because the fill is a mask change rather than a moving element, there's no additional motion to disable.

Other use cases

Once you understand masks, you'll start to see them everywhere. Here are two quick examples.

Read-only stars rating

Figure 12.4 - Final result: Star rating.

Stack two identical star rows and reveal the top row with a left-to-right mask driven by a percentage. Great for displaying ratings.

```
<div class="stars" style="--p: 70%">
  <div class="row row--bg" aria-hidden="true">★★★★★</div>
  <div class="row row--fg" aria-hidden="true">★★★★★</div>
</div>
```

```
.stars {
  position: relative;
  display: inline-grid;
}

.stars > * {
  grid-area: 1/1;
  font-size: 40px;
  letter-spacing: 4px;
}

.row--bg {
  color: #cbd5e1;
}
```

```
.row--fg {
  color: #f59e0b;
  -webkit-mask: linear-gradient(to right, #000 0, var(--p,0%), transparent 0);
  mask:         linear-gradient(to right, #000 0, var(--p,0%), transparent 0);
}
```

Link to the codepen: `https://codepen.io/theosoti/pen/bNVMNBp`.

Masked banner silhouette

Figure 12.5 - Final result: Svg covering an image.

Show a background photo only inside a PNG silhouette by masking a full-bleed pseudo-element. The content remains normal, the art is revealed through the mask.

```
<div class="banner">
  <div class="content">
    <h1>Great mask effect</h1>
  </div>
</div>
```

```
.banner {
  position: relative;
  height: 100vh;
}
```

```
/* The masked artwork lives behind as ::before */
.banner::before {
  content: "";
  position: absolute;
  inset: 0;
  z-index: -1;
  background-image: url("img.jpeg");
  background-size: cover;
  background-position: top;

  /* Key: reveal the photo only where the PNG is opaque */
  -webkit-mask-image: url(img.png);
  mask-image: url(img.png);
  mask-size: cover;
  mask-position: center;
}
```

Swap the PNG for any silhouette (logo, mascot, letterform). The photo never reflows, the mask simply decides what's visible.

Link to the codepen: `https://codepen.io/theosoti/pen/GgRgMMj`.

> Note
>
> ⓘ **Browser Compatibility (as of March 2026)**
>
> - CSS masks (`mask`, plus `-webkit-mask` for older WebKit/Safari): Supported in all modern browsers (~96.4%) (`https://caniuse.com/?search=mask`).
> - `-moz-range-thumb & -webkit-slider-thumb`: Combined support across modern browsers with around 92% (`https://caniuse.com/?search=-webkit-slider-thumb`)

Note

Key Takeaways

- Use two complementary masks that meet at a shared stop (`var(--pos)`) to reveal one layer while hiding the other.
- Keep the control native with a full-surface range, it stays accessible and gives you a value you can submit immediately.

Drive everything from a single custom property, your script only updates `--pos`.

Masks introduced a creative dimension to layout and effects, enabling reveals, cutouts, and overlays that once demanded complex solutions. They give you more control over how information is presented.

Next, let's return to usability with form validation.

13

CSS-Only Form Validation

Modern CSS lets you style validation states without JavaScript and without nagging users too early. `:valid` / `:invalid` always reflect constraint validity. The newer `:user-valid` / `:user-invalid` only flip after the user interacts (typing, blurring, or trying to submit). That means no "red errors" on untouched fields, while still updating instantly as the user corrects input.

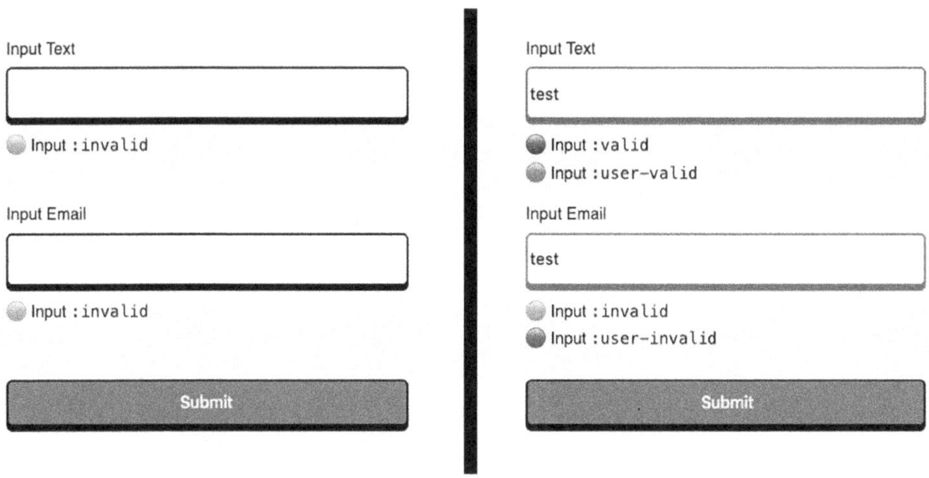

Figure 13.1 - Final result: A form with validation messages.

The Basic HTML

We'll use your exact markup: two inputs (text + email), each followed by a small state readout. The submit button is a normal `type="submit"`. Pressing it on an untouched invalid field also counts as user interaction for the `:user-*` selectors.

```
<form>
  <div class="field">
    <label for="input">Input Text</label>
    <input id="input" required="required" type="text" />
    <ul class="validation" role="list">
      <li data-matches="valid"> ● Input <code>:valid</code></li>
      <li data-matches="invalid">● Input <code>:invalid</code></li>
      <li data-matches="user-valid">● Input <code>:user-valid</code></li>
      <li data-matches="user-invalid">● Input <code>:user-invalid</code></li>
    </ul>
  </div>

  <div class="field">
    <label for="email">Input Email</label>
    <input id="email" required="required"
           type="email" pattern="[^@\\s]+@[^@\\s]+\\.[^@\\s]+" />
    <ul class="validation" role="list">
      <li data-matches="valid">● Input <code>:valid</code></li>
      <li data-matches="invalid"> ● Input <code>:invalid</code></li>
      <li data-matches="user-valid"> ● Input <code>:user-valid</code></li>
      <li data-matches="user-invalid">● Input <code>:user-invalid</code></li>
    </ul>
  </div>

  <div class="buttons">
    <input type="submit" value="Submit">
  </div>
</form>
```

Note

Note on constraints

The email field uses both `type="email"` and a `pattern`. The `pattern` adds an extra rule on top of the built-in email validity. Use it only if you truly need stricter formatting.

Base styling and a hidden message list

Start by giving inputs a neutral look and hide all messages by default. A CSS variable `--state-color` will be our single source of truth for borders and shadows.

```
/* messages start hidden */
.validation [data-matches] {
  display: none;
}

/* neutral input shell */
input {
  --state-color: black;     /* default color until a state matches */
  height: 45px;
  border: 2px solid var(--state-color);
  box-shadow: 0 5px 0 0 var(--state-color);
}
```

Messages will be revealed selectively when a given state matches. The field's color will be driven by the variable.

Color by "user" states (only after interaction)

Set the variable only when the user has interacted. This avoids red errors on untouched fields while still confirming success immediately once corrected.

```
input:user-valid {
  --state-color: green;
}

input:user-invalid {
```

```
  --state-color: red;
}
```

Behind the scenes, the browser tracks interaction: once the user edits or tries to submit, `:user-valid` / `:user-invalid` begin to participate. Required fields that are empty are not flagged as "user-invalid" until that interaction has happened.

Show messages for both classic and "user" validity

Use sibling selectors to reveal the right message under each input. The `:valid` / `:invalid` lines reflect current constraint validity. The `:user-*` lines reflect user-touched validity.

```
/* current constraint validity (always evaluates) */
input:valid + .validation [data-matches="valid"],
input:invalid + .validation [data-matches="invalid"] {
  display: block;
}

/* user-touched validity (only after interaction) */
input:user-valid + .validation [data-matches="user-valid"],
input:user-invalid + .validation [data-matches="user-invalid"] {
  display: block;
}
```

This split makes the learning demo explicit: you can see the difference between constraint validity and user-touched validity in real time. On a production UI you'd typically show just one friendly hint, not all four.

Link to the codepen: `https://codepen.io/theosoti/pen/ogNZzdJ`.

Always validate on submit

Everything in this chapter is UX. CSS (and even the browser's built-in validity UI) lives on the client and can be bypassed or altered. Treat `:user-valid` / `:user-invalid` as friendly guidance, not security. Always validate again on the server (and/or in a trusted API layer) before processing or storing data. Sanitize, normalize, and re-check constraints server-side.

Note

ⓘ **Browser Compatibility (as of March 2026)**

- `:valid` / `:invalid` have browser support of 96.7% (`https://caniuse.com/?search=%3Avalid`).
- `:user-valid` / `:user-invalid` have global support of 87% (`https://caniuse.com/?search=%3Auser-invalid`). Older browsers will simply ignore those selectors.
- You can gate enhancements with:

```
@supports selector(:user-invalid) {}.
```

Note

☑ **Key Takeaways**

- Use `:user-valid` / `:user-invalid` to show feedback after interaction. Keep `:valid` / `:invalid` for raw constraint state.
- Drive all styling from a single CSS variable like `--state-color` to keep rules simple.
- Reveal messages with sibling selectors. Consider `:has()` to style the field group when errors occur.
- Treat `:user-*` as progressive enhancement. Non-supporting browsers gracefully fall back to classic validity.
- Still validate on the server. CSS validation states improve UX, but they're not a security boundary or data contract.

We've now explored some of CSS's most powerful new capabilities. From animated borders to seamless page transitions, precise motion paths, and creative masking... Even form validation can now be handled directly with CSS. Together, these techniques show that modern CSS isn't just for presentation anymore, it's becoming a first-class tool for interaction and behavior.

But this is only the beginning. Beyond these power moves lies a new wave of features that are still emerging, reshaping what's possible on the web. In the next part, we'll take a glimpse into the future of CSS. Exploring experimental APIs and forward-looking patterns that push the boundaries of what you thought could be done without JavaScript.

Part 3

A Glimpse of the Future

CSS is evolving fast, and some of its most exciting powers are only just arriving in browsers. This final part is a look ahead: components and techniques that feel futuristic today, but will become everyday tools in the years to come. We'll see how to experiment with them now, add graceful fallbacks, and prepare for the moment when they're ready for production.

This part contains the following chapters:

- *Chapter 14, Scroll-Driven Animations*
- *Chapter 15, Native Popovers*
- *Chapter 16, Customized Selects*
- *Chapter 17, Anchor Positioning*
- *Chapter 18, Native CSS Carousels*
- *Chapter 19, And more to come...*

14

Scroll-Driven Animations

Normally, CSS animations run against a clock: you define a duration, and the browser advances keyframes as time passes. With scroll-driven animations, the "clock" is replaced by scroll position. As you move through the page, the browser maps your progress to the animation's progress.

These animations run off-thread, meaning they're handled by the browser's compositor (the graphics engine) instead of the main JavaScript thread. The benefit: smoother motion and less jank, because they don't compete with your page's scripts or layout work.

Figure 14.1 - Final result: Scroll indicator growing depending on the scroll of the page.

The Basic HTML Structure

We need a scrollable page and a place to show progress. The idea: a header that contains the progress bar, and a main area long enough to scroll.

```
<header>
  <h1>Scroll animations</h1>
  <div class="progress"></div>
</header>

<main>
  <!-- Your content -->
</main>
```

Here, `.progress` is the bar container. We'll draw the fixed background on `.progress` itself, and the moving fill with a `::before` pseudo-element so we don't need extra markup.

Draw the track

```
.progress {
  background: #000;
  height: 8px;
  position: relative;
}
```

This creates a solid black strip. `position: relative;` matters because it gives a positioning context for the pseudo-element we'll add next. Think of it as the "empty track" that the filling bar will sit on top of.

Add the fill

```
.progress::before {
  content: '';
  position: absolute;
  background: #55ad9b;
  width: 100%;
  height: 8px;

  transform: scaleX(0);
```

```
  transform-origin: left;
}
```

Here, the pseudo-element is the filling bar. Instead of starting at `width: 0`, we set `width: 100%` and shrink it with `scaleX(0)`.

- `transform: scaleX(0)` compresses it to nothing.
- `transform-origin: left` ensures it expands outward from the left edge.

This way we animate only a transform, which is GPU-friendly and avoids layout shifts.

Define the animation

```
@keyframes grow {
  to {
    transform: scaleX(1);
  }
}
```

This animation scales the bar from nothing (`scaleX(0)`) to its full width (`scaleX(1)`).

Link animation to scroll

```
.progress:before {
  ...
  animation: grow linear both;  /* play the keyframes */
  animation-timeline: scroll(); /* let page scroll drive progress */
}
```

Here we apply the grow keyframes and then change their "clock" with `animation-timeline: scroll()`. Here the browser maps the animation progress to the page's scroll position. The result is simple to understand: when you're at the top of the page the bar is collapsed, when you reach the bottom it has expanded fully, and in between its scale matches your exact scroll progress.

Link to the codepen: `https://codepen.io/theosoti/pen/ExqEyBO`.

Other use cases:

Coverflow-on-scroll (horizontal view timeline)

Figure 14.2 - Final result: scrolling horizontally makes the slides move and grow.

Scroll horizontally through a list of cards, and each one rotates and scales as it crosses the viewport center.

```
<main>
  <ul>
    <li><img src="img.png" width="300" height="300" alt="album" /></li>
    <li><img src="img.png" width="300" height="300" alt="album" /></li>
    <li><img src="img.png" width="300" height="300" alt="album" /></li>
    <!-- ...repeat... -->
  </ul>
</main>
```

```
li {
  animation: linear adjust-z-index both;
  animation-timeline: view(inline);
}

img {
  animation: linear rotate-cover both;
  animation-timeline: view(inline);
}
```

The trick is `view(inline)`: instead of page scroll, the animation progress is tied to each element's horizontal journey. One animation adjusts stacking so the middle card sits on top, while the other rotates and scales the card as it moves across the screen.

Link to the codepen: `https://codepen.io/theosoti/pen/NPGoeEy`.

Section image reveal

You can also make elements appear gradually as they scroll into view.

Figure 14.3 - Final result: Scrolling on the page makes the image appear/disapear.

```
<article>
  <p>Some content</p>
  <img src="https://picsum.photos/id/400/600/300" alt="placeholder" />
  <p>Some content</p>
  <img src="https://picsum.photos/id/500/600/300" alt="placeholder" />
  <p>Some content</p>
</article>
```

```
img {
  position: relative;
  left: -200px;
  opacity: 0;
```

```
  animation: fadeIn linear forwards;
  animation-timeline: view(); /* starts on entry, ends on exit */
  animation-range-start: 100px; /* begin 100px after entry */
  animation-range-end: 500px; /* finish around mid-viewport */
}

@keyframes fadeIn {
  to {
    opacity: 1;
    left: 0;
  }
}
```

Here, `view()` ties the animation to the image's journey through the viewport. The range (`100px → 500px`) delays the effect so the image doesn't appear right at the edge, but instead fades and slides into place more smoothly as you scroll down.

Link to the codepen: `https://codepen.io/theosoti/pen/QWRgbmR`.

And there are a lot of other use cases and demos you can find on Scroll Driven Animation (`https://scroll-driven-animations.style/`).

Note

ⓘ Browser Compatibility (as of March 2026)

- Scroll-driven animations (`animation-timeline: scroll()` / `view()`, plus `animation-range`) work in current Chrome/Edge. Global browser support of ~78% (`https://caniuse.com/?search=animation-timeline`).
- Use `@supports` so unsupported browsers just see a static track:

```
@supports (animation-timeline: scroll()) {
  .progress:before {
    animation: grow linear forwards;
    animation-timeline: scroll();
  }
}
```

- There are community polyfills that bring ScrollTimeline/ViewTimeline to more browsers (JavaScript-driven), e.g. flackr/scroll-timeline (`https://github.com/flackr/scroll-timeline`). Use only if the effect is critical and you accept the JS cost.

Note

☑ **Key Takeaways**

- You're not changing the animation, you're changing the clock that drives it.
- `animation-timeline: scroll()` maps page scroll to keyframe progress, no duration required.
- Your animation stays tiny: one track, one pseudo-element, one keyframe block.
- Use `@supports` and design so the page reads fine without the animation, enhanced when supported.

Scroll-driven animations showed how CSS can now synchronize effects directly with the user's scrolling, making layouts feel dynamic and alive without scripting. It's a feature that connects motion to intent in a natural way.

Next, let's move on to overlays and see how popovers are now handled natively in the browser.

15

Native Popovers

Menus, tooltips, callouts... these are everywhere in web interfaces. But historically, building them has been messy: you had to wire up `aria-` attributes, handle keyboard focus, manage z-index stacking, and write JavaScript for open/close toggles and outside-click dismissal.

The Popover API solves all of that. With just two HTML attributes, you get:

- Automatic top-layer stacking (always on top)
- Focus management (focus moves inside when opened, returns when closed)
- Light-dismiss (ESC key and outside clicks close it)
- Clean, accessible behavior with no JavaScript

You then layer CSS on top for design. No library, no boilerplate.

Figure 15.1 - Final result: Left - no popover. Right - a showing popover.

The Basic HTML Structure

Every popover needs two parts:

1. A trigger element (often a button)
2. A popover element (any element with the `popover` attribute)

```
<button popovertarget="more">More options</button>

<div id="more" popover>
  <p>Native popover 👋</p>
</div>
```

Here's what's happening:

- The button has `popovertarget="more"`. This wires it to the element with `id="more"`.
- The `<div popover>` is now a real popover.
- When the button is clicked, the browser shows/hides the popover automatically.

The browser also takes care of focus (moving it into the popover) and light-dismiss (closing on outside click or *Esc*). You don't need a single line of JavaScript for those behaviors.

Minimal skin (make it look like a card)

A popover is just another DOM element. To make it feel like a card, you add ordinary CSS:

```
[popover] {
  padding: .75rem 1rem;
  border: 1px solid #e5e7eb;
  border-radius: .5rem;
  background: #fff;
  box-shadow: 0 10px 30px rgb(0 0 0 / .12);
}
```

This gives it a lightweight, elevated style.

> Note
>
> **ⓘ Notice**
>
> You don't need to mess with `position`, `inset`, or `margin`. Placement is handled by the browser's top-layer system. If you override it, you risk breaking the built-in logic.

Built-in close control

You'll often want the popover to close from inside (e.g. a "X" button). That's also built-in:

```
<div id="more" popover>
  <p>Native popover 👋</p>
  <button popovertarget="more" popovertargetaction="hide" aria-label="Close">X</
button>
</div>
```

The `popovertarget` attribute links this button to the same popover. Whereas the `popovertargetaction` attribute controls the behavior:

- `toggle` (default) → open if closed, close if open
- `show` → always open it
- `hide` → always close it

This is declarative control, the browser handles state changes without event listeners or scripts.

Adding animation

By default, popovers just "pop" in and out. That's functional, but not polished. To animate them, you define both a closed state and an open state, then let CSS transitions do the rest.

```
/* add to your base rule */
[popover] {
  transform: translateY(-50px);
  opacity: 0;
  transition: transform 0.5s, opacity 0.5s, display 0.5s;
  transition-behavior: allow-discrete; /* enables closing animation */
}

/* add to your open-state rule */
[popover]:popover-open {
  transform: translateY(0);
  opacity: 1;

  /* starting values for the entry transition */
  @starting-style {
```

```
    transform: translateY(-50px);
    opacity: 0;
  }
}
```

What's happening here:

- In the closed state, the popover is shifted up and fully transparent.
- When opened (`:popover-open`), it moves into place and fades in.
- `@starting-style` defines the frame where the opening transition begins.
- `transition-behavior: allow-discrete` allows the closing animation to play before the popover is removed from the DOM flow.

The result: a smooth slide-and-fade both on entry and exit

Here's a Codepen to see the demo: `https://codepen.io/theosoti/pen/KwdbLYd`.

> Note
>
> ⚠ **Tips & troubleshooting**
>
> - For robust placement through scroll/resize, pair popovers with CSS anchor positioning (`anchor()`) from our previous chapter. The two APIs are designed to work together.
> - Any number of buttons can target the same popover by `id`. Each can choose `show | hide | toggle`.
> - JS hooks (optional): `showPopover()`, `hidePopover()`, `togglePopover()` and the `beforetoggle/toggle` events are available if you need side effects

Another Use Case: Off-Canvas Menu

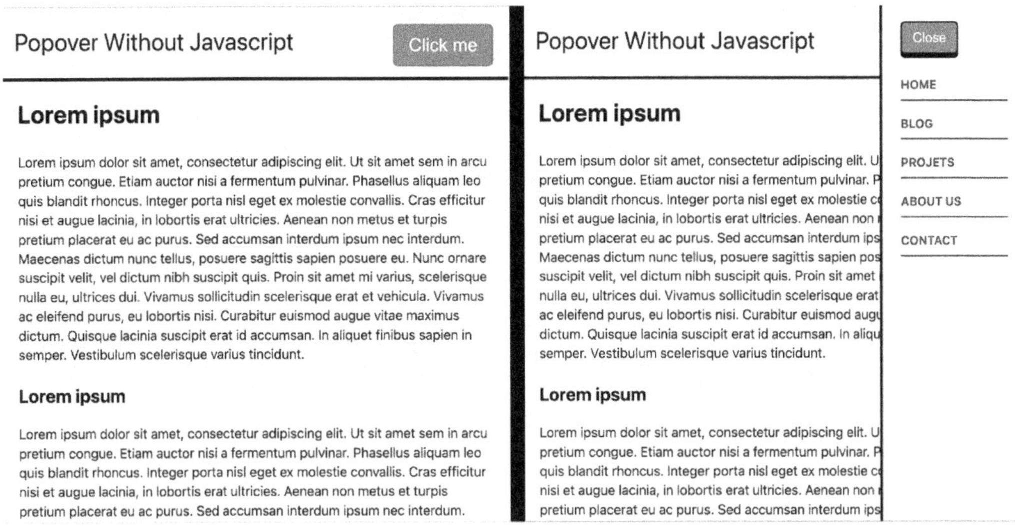

Figure 15.2 - Final result: a whole menu appearing on the right like a drawer.

Use a popover as a right-hand off-canvas menu. One button shows the menu, a close button inside hides it. The slide is pure CSS with a discrete transition for a smooth exit.

```
<button popovertarget="navigation" popovertargetaction="show">
  Menu
</button>

<nav popover id="navigation">
  <button popovertarget="navigation" popovertargetaction="hide">
    Close
  </button>
  <ul>
    <li><a href="#">HOME</a></li>
    <li><a href="#">BLOG</a></li>
    <li><a href="#">...</a></li>
  </ul>
</nav>
```

```
#navigation {
  height: 100vh;
  width: 200px;
  margin-left: auto; /* dock to the right */
  transition: transform .2s ease-out, opacity .2s ease-out, display .2s;

  /* lets the close animate */
  transition-behavior: allow-discrete;

  /* closed state */
  opacity: 0;
  transform: translateX(200px);
}

/* open state */
#navigation:popover-open {
  transform: translateX(0);
  opacity: 1;

  @starting-style {
    /* starting values for the entry transition */
    transform: translateX(200px);
    opacity: 0;
  }
}

/* optional: dim the page while open */
#mobile-navigation::backdrop {
  background: rgb(0 0 0 / .35);
}
```

No JavaScript required. The Popover API handles focus and light-dismiss. Add the `::backdrop` rule if you want a soft overlay behind the menu.

Here's a Codepen to see the demo: `https://codepen.io/theosoti/pen/ZENpowe`.

Note

ⓘ **Browser Compatibility (as of March 2026)**

- Anchors (`:popover-open`, `popover`, `popovertargetaction` and `popovertarget`) work in all modern browsers. Global browser support of ~87.5% (`https://caniuse.com/?search=%3Apopover-open`).
- `transition-behavior: allow-discrete` have a browser support of 86.7% (`https://caniuse.com/mdn-css_properties_transition-behavior_allow-discrete`).
- Progressive enhancement: In older browsers, attributes are ignored and content renders inline. Gate styles with:

```
@supports selector(:popover-open) {
  /* popover styles */  }
```

Note

☑ **Key Takeaways**

- Add `popover` to any element; control it from a button with `popovertarget` (+ optional `popovertargetaction`).
- Style and place the popover in `:popover-open`, override the User Agent's centered default.
- Animate correctly with `@starting-style` and a discrete `display` transition so entry/exit both feel smooth.
- Combine with anchor positioning for bulletproof tethering; use JS only for advanced behaviors.

Popovers showed how overlays can be displayed and dismissed with minimal code while keeping accessibility built in.

Next, let's revisit form controls and learn how to restyle the `<select>` element natively.

16

Customized Selects

Native selects are accessible and keyboard-friendly, but very hard to style. Most teams end up replacing them with custom "fake" dropdowns built in JavaScript. But it often meant losing built-in accessibility, focus management, and OS consistency.

That era is ending. The Customizable Select model lets you style every part of a real `<select>` like the button face, the arrow, the dropdown, and the checkmark, while keeping native semantics and behavior intact.

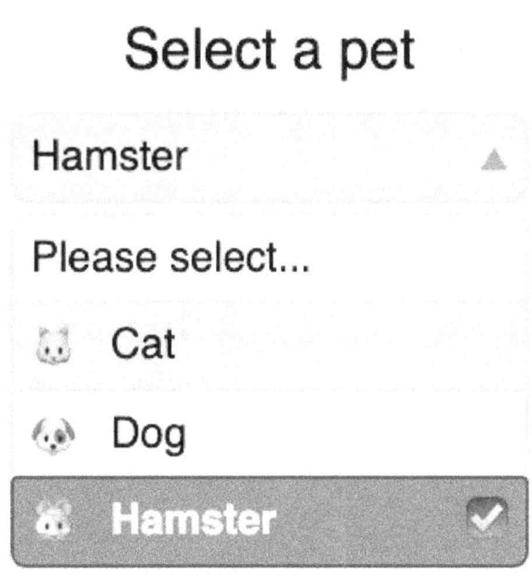

Figure 16.1 - Final result: a select component full CSS.

The Basic HTML Structure

Start with a real `<select>`. Inside it, place a `<button>` as the first child. That button becomes the visible "closed" face of the select. Inside the button, add `<selectedcontent>`, this automatically mirrors the currently chosen `<option>`.

```
<label for="pet">Select a pet</label>
<select id="pet">
  <button>
    <selectedcontent></selectedcontent>
  </button>

  <option value="">Please select...</option>
  <option value="cat">
    <span class="icon" aria-hidden="true">🐱</span>
    <span class="label">Cat</span>
  </option>
  <option value="dog">
    <span class="icon" aria-hidden="true">🐶</span>
    <span class="label">Dog</span>
  </option>
  <option value="hamster">
    <span class="icon" aria-hidden="true">🐹</span>
    <span class="label">Hamster</span>
  </option>
</select>
```

Why this works:

- In the customizable select model, the first child button replaces the default face.
- `<selectedcontent>` acts as a live mirror, the browser copies the chosen option's content into it automatically.
- In non-supporting browsers, the extra children are ignored. You get a classic `<select>` with full functionality.

That makes this naturally progressive: one markup, two behaviors depending on browser support.

Opting In

To enable customization, you opt in with:

```
select,
::picker(select) {
  appearance: base-select; /* opt-in to the customizable select model */
}
```

This removes the OS chrome but keeps semantics, keyboard UX, and screen reader behavior. You can apply it only to the button if you prefer the native dropdown, or to both for full styling control.

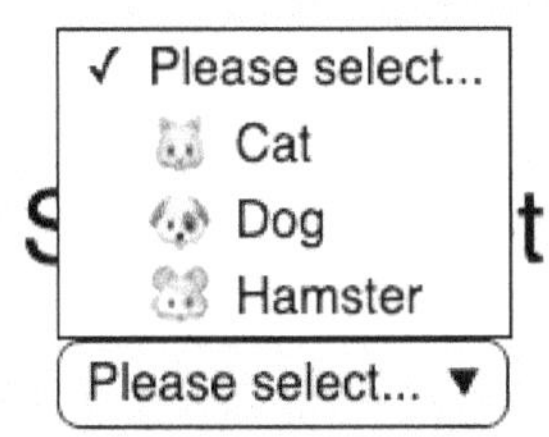

Figure 16.2 - Result with just this line of CSS.

Styling the Button Face

Once you've opted in, the `<select>` is yours to style. Treat it like any other button:

```
select {
  display: inline-block;
  border: 2px solid #d1d5db;
  background: #f3f4f6;
  padding: .5rem .75rem;
  border-radius: .5rem;
  transition: background .25s;
}
```

```
select:hover,
select:focus {
  background: #e5e7eb;
}
```

At this point you have a face that looks and feels like the rest of your UI while still being a genuine form control. The browser continues to announce it correctly and submit its value.

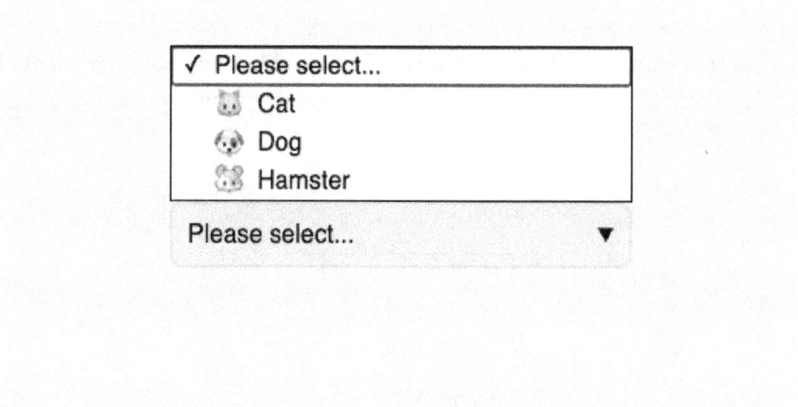

Figure 16.3 - The button is now styled.

Customizing the Arrow

The arrow is no longer a black box. The `::picker-icon` pseudo-element targets the built-in icon inside the face. You can recolor it, resize it, or animate it to reflect the control's state using `:open`.

```
select::picker-icon {
  color: #6b7280;
  transition: rotate .3s;
}

select:open::picker-icon {
  rotate: 180deg;  /* flips when the list is open */
}
```

The flip is a small touch, but it signals state change without scripting. If your system uses different indicators (chevrons, carets), you can swap visuals globally here rather than per component.

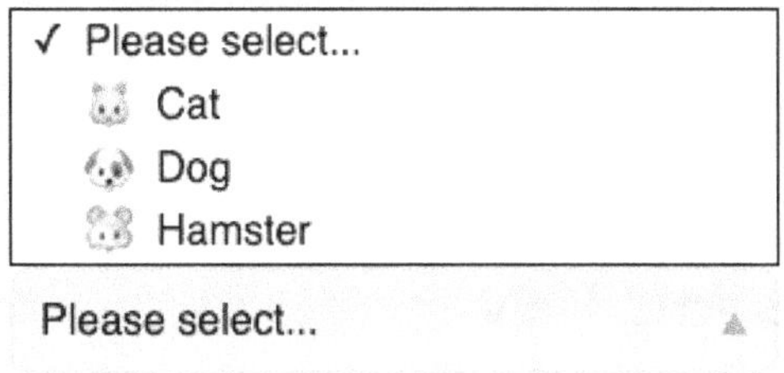

Figure 16.4 - The arrow is changed and responsive with the select state (open/closed).

Styling the Dropdown and Its Options

The popup is the *picker* and is targetable as `::picker(select)`. Inside it, each `<option>` is stylable. The customizable model allows options to participate in layout (flex is common), which means text and small icons align cleanly without hacks.

```
/* the popup surface */
::picker(select) {
  border: none;  /* remove default black border */
  padding: 0;
}

/* each option row */
option {
  display: flex;
  align-items: center;
  gap: .5rem;
  border: 2px solid #d1d5db;
  background: #f9fafb;
  padding: .5rem .75rem;
}

option:hover,
option:focus {
```

```
  background: #e5e7eb;
}
```

This is where a lot of historical "custom dropdown" code disappears. Hover and focus styling is now just CSS. Keyboard navigation and type-ahead continue to work because the element is still a select.

Keeping the Button Tidy

Often your options contain icons or secondary text, but the face should remain compact. Because `<selectedcontent>` mirrors the chosen option, you can selectively hide pieces *only* in the mirrored view while leaving them visible in the list.

```
selectedcontent .icon {
  display: none;
}
```

The result: rich options in the popup, a clean label in the face. If you do want the icon in the face, remove that rule and the mirror will include it automatically.

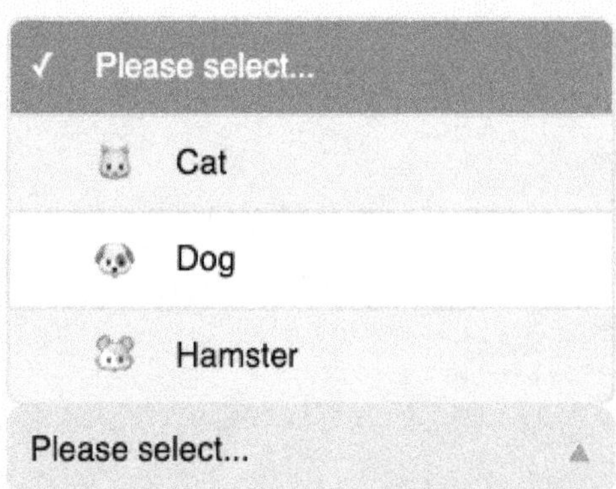

Figure 16.5 - Already looking good!

Style the selected option and its checkmark

Native selects show an affordance next to the active choice. In the customizable model, `:checked` styles the chosen option and `::checkmark` controls the marker's placement and appearance.

```
option:checked {
  font-weight: 700;
}

option::checkmark {
  order: 1; /* move the marker to the end of the row */
  margin-left: auto;
  content: "☑"; /* swap the icon if you like */
}
```

The checkmark content is purely visual; assistive tech announces the selection based on the native control, not the decoration. This keeps you free to change the icon without compromising accessibility.

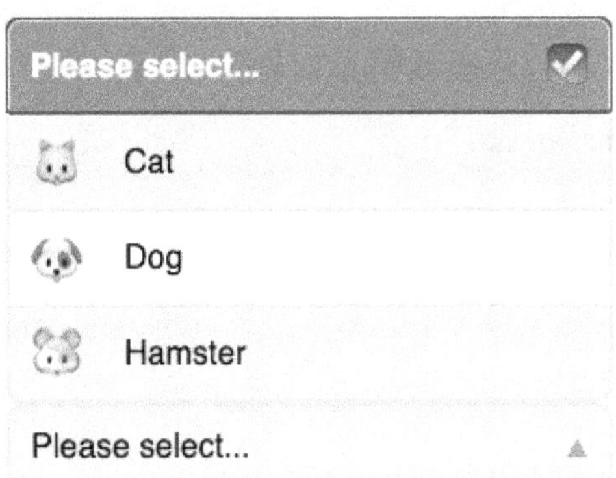

Figure 16.6 - Now even the checkmark is customized.

Here's a Codepen to see the demo: `https://codepen.io/theosoti/pen/zxvMMbe`.

Note

⚠ **Tips & troubleshooting**

- Some frameworks block these features or mis-hydrate when a `<button>` appears inside `<select>`. If you SSR, test hydration or guard with `@supports`.
- You can style just the button and leave the OS dropdown by applying `appearance: base-select` only to `select`, not `::picker(select)`.
- The picker is a popover anchored to its button. You can animate with `:popover-open` or reposition with anchor positioning if needed.

Note

ⓘ **Browser Compatibility (as of March 2026)**

- Customizable Select (`appearance: base-select`, `::picker`, `<selectedcontent>`, `::checkmark`, and `::picker-icon`) work in current Chrome/Edge. Global browser support of ~68.7% (`https://caniuse.com/?search=appearance%3A%20base-select`).
- Gating with `@supports`:

```
@supports (appearance: base-select) {
  select,
  ::picker(select) {
    appearance: base-select;
  }
  /* ...your customizable rules here... */
}
```

- Non-supporting browsers ignore the new bits and fall back to a classic select, your form still works

Note

Key Takeaways

- No more `appearance: none`, keep the real `<select>` and style it via `appearance: base-select` and friends.
- Target the button (the closed state), the arrow (`::picker-icon`), the dropdown (`::picker(select)`), the selected option (`:checked`), and the checkmark (`::checkmark`). All with plain CSS.
- It's progressive by design: unsupported browsers see a normal select, supporting ones get the custom skin with native a11y intact.

Styling selects proved that even the most basic form controls can be aligned with your design system using modern CSS. It keeps interfaces consistent while preserving accessibility.

Next, let's explore precision placement with anchors.

17

Anchor Positioning

Tooltips, dropdowns, popovers... these UI elements have always been tricky. Traditionally you had to measure offsets with JavaScript or rely on positioning libraries. Modern CSS now solves this elegantly with anchor positioning.

With this feature, you can "tether" one element to another: name an anchor (like a button) and position another element (like a tooltip) relative to it using the `anchor()` function. No manual math, no DOM measurements, the browser does the work, keeps it responsive, and even flips placement when there's not enough space.

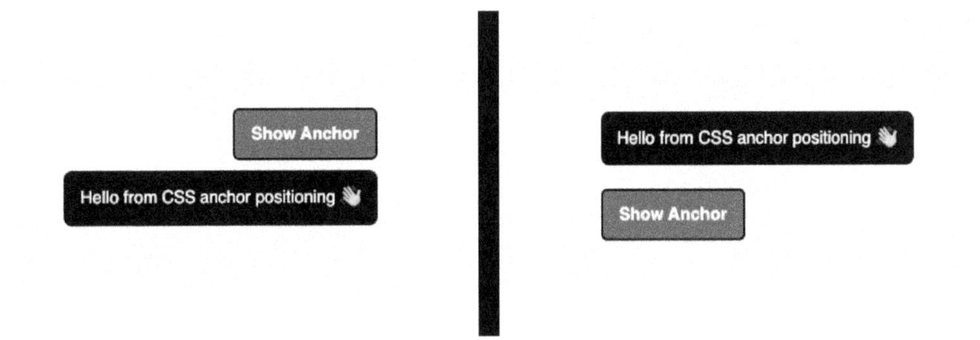

Figure 17.1 - Final result: automatically adjusting anchor.

The Basic HTML Structure

Clean and semantic: a button (the anchor) and a tooltip.

```
<button class="btn" aria-describedby="tip">More options</button>
```

```
<div class="tip" id="tip" role="tooltip">
    Hello from CSS anchor positioning 👋</div>
```

- The button is our anchor.
- The tooltip points to it with `aria-describedby` for accessibility.
- No wrappers or helper containers needed, the magic happens in CSS.

Declaring the Anchor

To use an element as a reference point, you must give it a name with the `anchor-name` property:

```
.btn {
  anchor-name: --btn; /* this can be targeted by anchored elements */
}
```

This is like putting a label on the button. Later, any other element (tooltip, dropdown, etc.) can say: "Stick to the anchor called `--btn`."

The double dashes are just a naming convention (like custom properties), you can call it `--trigger`, `--menu`, or anything you like.

Associating the Tooltip

Now we need to tell the tooltip which anchor to follow. That's done with `position-anchor`.

```
.tip {
  position: absolute;         /* required for anchor positioning */
  position-anchor: --btn;     /* bind to the button by name */
  z-index: 10;

  /* visual skin (just for the demo) */
  padding: .5rem .75rem;
  background: #111;
  color: white;
  border-radius: .5rem;
}
```

Two rules make anchoring work:

1. The element must be positioned (`absolute` or `fixed`), otherwise it has nothing to "lock" against.
2. It must declare which anchor it belongs to with `position-anchor`.

Think of it like this: "I'm absolutely positioned... but not relative to the container, I'm relative to the anchor named `--btn`."

Placing with anchor()

By default, the tooltip would stack in the top-left corner of the anchor. To control the exact relationship, we use the `anchor()` function:

```
.tip {
  /* vertical: place top edge just below the anchor's bottom */
  top:  calc(anchor(bottom) + 8px);

  /* horizontal: center on the anchor */
  left: anchor(left);
}
```

- `anchor(bottom)` gives the position of the button's bottom edge.
- `anchor(left)` gives the left edge.
- You can also use `anchor(top)`, `anchor(right)`, or even `anchor(center)` for centering.

Because `anchor()` returns a length, you can combine it with `calc()` to fine-tune gaps, offsets, or centering math.

Avoiding Clipping with Fallbacks

What if the button is near the bottom of the screen and there's no room for the tooltip? You can provide backup strategies:

```
.tip {
  position-try: flip-block flip-inline; /* try above, then left/right if needed */
}
```

- `flip-block` = if there's no space below, try placing it above.
- `flip-inline` = if there's no space horizontally, nudge left or right.

This gives tooltips and dropdowns resilience without JavaScript. The browser does the smart positioning for you.

Matching the Anchor's Width (Optional)

Dropdown menus often need to match their trigger's width. You can do that too:

```
.tip {
  inline-size: anchor-size(width); /* size relative to the anchor's width */
}
```

- `anchor-size(width)` returns the anchor's width as a usable length.
- There's also `anchor-size(height)` for vertical alignment cases.
- Since it's a length, you can `calc()` with it to add caps, max-widths, or margins.

This is perfect for dropdown menus, autocomplete panels, or tooltips that should feel visually tied to their trigger.

Here's a Codepen to see the demo: `https://codepen.io/theosoti/pen/dPYwLMP`

> Note
>
> ⚠ **Tips & troubleshooting**
>
> - `anchor()` is valid inside inset properties (`top`/`left`/`right`/`bottom` and logical variants). If you put a horizontal side in a vertical inset (or vice versa), the fallback value (if any) is used. Prefer logical values for i18n.
> - Add gaps with `calc(anchor(...) + 8px)` or plain margins (e.g., `margin-top: 8px` when anchoring below).
> - You can reference different named anchors on different sides (e.g., top to A, left to B) but the element associates (scrolls/hides with) a single `position-anchor`.

Note

ⓘ **Browser Compatibility (as of March 2026)**

- Anchors (`anchor()`, `anchor-name`, `position-anchor`, `anchor-size()`, and `position-try`) work in current Chrome/Edge. Global browser support of ~76.6% (`https://caniuse.com/?search=anchor()`).
- Gate styles so non-supporting browsers get a normal, usable UI:

```
@supports (anchor-name: --btn) {
  .btn {
    anchor-name: --btn;
  }

  .tip {
    position: absolute;
    position-anchor: --btn;
    top: calc(anchor(bottom) + 8px);
    left: calc(anchor(center) - 50%);
  }
}
```

- Content still works without anchoring. You just won't get the tethered placement

Note

☑ **Key Takeaways**

- Name an anchor, associate a positioned element, and place it with `anchor()`
- `anchor()` returns a length, so you can `calc()` spacing and centering. Use logical sides for writing-mode friendliness.
- Fallbacks with `position-try` keep popovers/tooltips visible by flipping when they'd overflow.

- `anchor-size()` lets you size the popup relative to the anchor (e.g., match trigger width).
- Guard with `@supports` and design for a graceful static layout when unsupported.

Anchor positioning showed how elements can stay neatly attached to their triggers with pure CSS, even as layouts shift. It's a simple, resilient way to manage menus and tooltips.

Now let's look at a classic: building a carousel entirely in CSS.

18

Native CSS Carousels

Browsers can now generate real carousel controls (buttons + markers) that you style, while scroll-snap gives you the paginated feel. Ship the snap-only baseline everywhere, then layer the new bits as progressive enhancement.

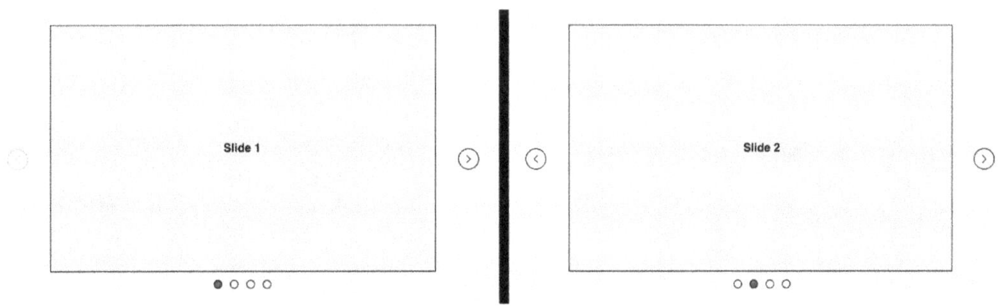

Figure 18.1 - Final result: a fully functioning carousel.

The Basic HTML Structure

A plain list becomes a carousel once we add CSS.

```
<ul class="carousel">
  <li><h3>Slide 1</h3></li>
  <li><h3>Slide 2</h3></li>
  <li><h3>Slide 3</h3></li>
  <li><h3>Slide 4</h3></li>
</ul>
```

Short, semantic markup keeps the fallback great: without the new features, users still swipe/ scroll a simple horizontal list.

Lay out the track

```
.carousel {
  display: flex;
  gap: 4em;
  padding: 1em;
  width: 800px;
  height: 500px;
  margin: auto;

  /* scrolling + pagination */
  overflow-x: hidden;
  scroll-behavior: smooth;
  scroll-snap-type: x mandatory;
  overscroll-behavior-x: contain;
}

.carousel > li {
  list-style: none;
  flex: 0 0 100%;
  background: #eee;
  border: 2px solid #000;
  scroll-snap-align: center;

  /* center the slide content */
  display: flex;
  align-items: center;
  justify-content: center;
}
```

Here the list becomes a snap container (`scroll-snap-type: x mandatory`) so each gesture lands on a defined stop, and each slide declares where it should settle (`scroll-snap-align: center`).

We've also enabled `scroll-behavior: smooth`, which gives a gentle glide for programmatic navigation (we'll trigger that with markers and arrows later). `overflow-x: hidden` creates the scroll container without exposing a rail. Users won't drag the track, but the generated controls will still paginate it. If you want both drag and controls, swap to `overflow-x: scroll.`

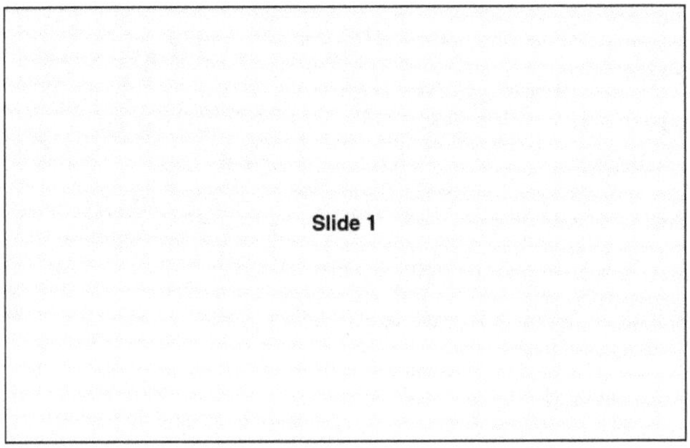

Figure 18.2 - Step 1: all slides are hidden, no buttons/navigation yet.

Add pagination dots

Turn on a scroll-marker group and generate one marker per slide. The browser wires them up like anchors: click a dot → scroll to that slide. Style them as you like.

```
/* turn on & position the marker group */
.carousel {
  scroll-marker-group: after;
  anchor-name: --carousel;
}

.carousel::scroll-marker-group {
  position: absolute;
  position-anchor: --carousel;
  top: calc(anchor(bottom));

  display: flex;
  justify-content: center;
  gap: 1em;
  inset-inline: 0;
}
```

```
/* one dot per slide */
.carousel > li::scroll-marker {
  content: "";
  inline-size: 14px;
  block-size: 14px;
  border-radius: 50%;
  border: 2px solid #000;
  background: transparent;
  color: green;                    /* drives the "filled" color */
}

.carousel > li::scroll-marker:target-current {
  background: currentColor;
}
```

`scroll-marker-group` is a property you turn on on the scroll container. It causes the browser to generate a `::scroll-marker-group` box either before or after the scroller in the visual and tab order.

Inside that group, each slide can generate its own `::scroll-marker` when you set `content`, activate a marker and the browser scrolls the container to its originating slide.
The `:target-current` pseudo-class matches the active marker so the "filled" state becomes a one-liner.

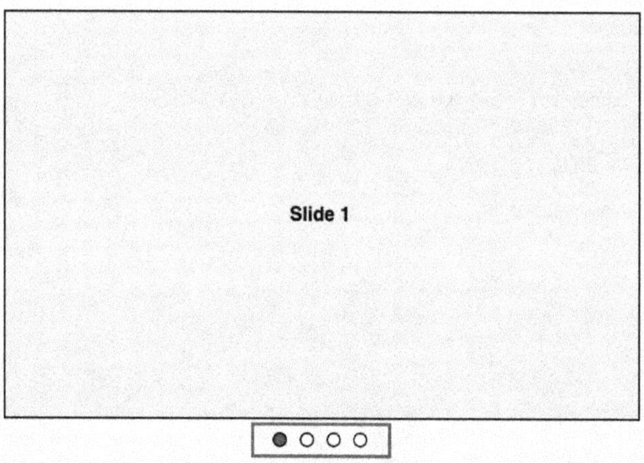

Figure 18.3 - Final result: navigation is showing and already working.

Add navigation arrows

`::scroll-button()` generates real, accessible previous/next buttons inside the scroll container when `content` isn't none.

```
.carousel::scroll-button(*) {
  position: absolute;
  text-align: center;
  position-anchor: --carousel;

  inline-size: 44px;
  block-size: 44px;

  border-radius: 50%;
  background: #fff;
  cursor: pointer;
  border: 2px solid #000;
}

.carousel::scroll-button(left) {
  content: "<";
  right: calc(anchor(left) + 1em);
  top: calc(anchor(center));
}

.carousel::scroll-button(right) {
  content: ">";
  left: calc(anchor(right) + 1em);
  top: calc(anchor(center));
}

.carousel::scroll-button(*):disabled {
  opacity: 0.35;
  cursor: default;
}
```

`::scroll-button()` generates real previous/next buttons inside the scroller as soon as `content` isn't none. The browser wires behavior and disables them at the ends, you handle visuals. Anchor positioning keeps them glued to the track across breakpoints. The track exposes `anchor-name: --carousel`, the buttons tether with `position-anchor: --carousel`, and `anchor()` gives you resilient placement.

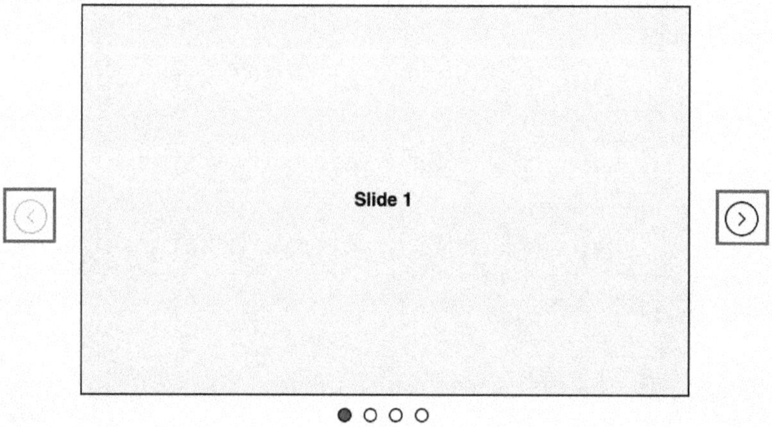

Figure 18.4 - Arrows are showing and also working.

Here's a Codepen to see the demo: `https://codepen.io/theosoti/pen/QwjoKgM`.

Note

ⓘ Browser Compatibility (as of March 2026)

- `scroll-snap` has a global browser support of ~95.4% (`https://caniuse.com/?search=scroll-snap`).
- `::scroll-button`, `::scroll-marker` and `::scroll-marker-group` have a global browser support of ~68.7% (`https://caniuse.com/?search=%3A%3Ascroll-button`).
- Gating with `@supports`:

```
@supports selector(::scroll-button(*)) and
          selector(::scroll-marker) and
          selector(::scroll-marker-group) {
  .carousel {
    /* your style */
  }
}
```

Note

☑ **Key Takeaways**

- Start with scroll-snap. It gives you pagination for free.
- Add buttons and markers by generating them in CSS, the browser wires up behavior and accessibility.
- Use anchor positioning so controls stay glued to the track as layouts change.
- Ship as progressive enhancement until support broadens. Your carousel is still great without the extras.

19

And more to come...

A handful of features are taking shape in specs and preview builds that could simplify whole classes of problems. They're not production-ready yet, but they're worth tracking and trying behind flags to shape the standards. Below you'll find what each feature is with a tiny example.

Native custom functions and mixins

The CSS Working Group published a Functions & Mixins draft. You can define your own dashed functions with `@function` and return computed values right inside CSS. Mixins (rule-level reuse) are planned in the same module but are not yet defined in the draft. Try custom functions today in experimental builds.

```
/* Define a dashed custom function that multiplies spacing */
@function --space(--n <number> : 1) {
  result: calc(1rem * var(--n));
}

.card {
  /* Use the function like any other value */
  padding: --space(1.5);
}

/* Progressive enhancement: only run where functions parse */
@supports (padding: --space(2)) {
  .stack > * {
    margin-block-start: --space(1);
  }
}
```

This behaves like "parameterized custom properties", evaluated at the point of use. Great for consistent spacing, shadows, and derived values without a preprocessor.

Inline conditionals with if()

`if()` lets a single property's value vary based on a style query, media query, or feature query, without wrapping the whole block in `@media`/`@supports`. It's explicitly marked experimental / limited availability on MDN, so treat it as progressive enhancement.

```
/* Fallback first, then override with if() where supported */
.card {
  padding: 1rem;
}

.card {
  padding: if(media(width < 700px): .75rem; else: 1.25rem);
}

/* Feature-query example inside if() */
.button {
  color: if(supports(color: lch(55% 60 310)): lch(55% 60 310);
    else: rgb(32 32 32));
}
```

Because non-supporting browsers ignore the `if()` value, you keep a safe baseline via the preceding declaration.

Masonry-style layout via Item Flow

"Item Flow" is a proposal to unify placement across Flexbox and Grid and, crucially, to make masonry a first-class variant of Grid. It's still being debated; the latest WebKit posts show what the syntax might look like and why.

```
/* Proposal sketch from WebKit's write-up */
.gallery {
  display: grid;
  grid-template-columns: repeat(auto-fill, minmax(14rem, 1fr));
  item-flow: row collapse;    /* collapse rows → classic masonry "waterfall" */
  gap: 1rem;
}
```

Don't ship this yet. It's for experimentation and feedback to the CSSWG.

True randomness with random()

A CSS `random()` function is emerging that returns random values or choices right in CSS. Great for offsets, delays, subtle texture, etc. Safari Technology Preview has an early implementation.

```
/* Safari Technology Preview today; gate carefully */
@supports (left: random(0px, 1px)) {
  .confetti > i {
    animation-delay: random(0ms, 600ms, 50ms); /* stepped randomness */
    translate: random(-30vw, 30vw) random(-10vh, 10vh);
  }
}
```

Use sparingly: it's experimental and non-deterministic by definition.

sibling-index() and sibling-count()

These functions return an element's 1-based index among siblings and the total siblings count—integers you can drop into `calc()`, timing, or sizes. They're shipping in Chrome/Edge 138+; other engines are evaluating.

```
/***** Simple stagger *****/
.card {
  animation: fade-up 400ms ease both;
  animation-delay: calc((sibling-index() - 1) * 80ms);
}

/***** Scale cards based on how many are in a row *****/
.row > .card {
  --n: sibling-count();
  flex-basis: calc(100% / var(--n));
}

/* Gate usage so older browsers ignore the fancy bits */
@supports (z-index: sibling-index()) {
  .card {
    outline-offset: calc(2px * sibling-index());
  }
}
```

```
@keyframes fade-up {
  from {
    opacity: 0;
    translate: 0 10px;
  }
}
```

This is fantastic for pure-CSS staggers and dynamic sizing without extra classes.

More powerful attr()

The classic `attr()` could only feed strings into `content`. The redesigned `attr()` lets you read an element's attribute, cast it to a type, and use it on any CSS property like numbers, colors, lengths, idents, percentages, even unitized values like `deg` and `px`. In Chrome 133+ this ships broadly. Other engines are exploring it, so treat it as progressive enhancement for now.

```
<div class="chip" data-accent="#8b5cf6" data-w="16" data-rot="-6"></div>
```

```
/* Baseline styles */
.chip {
  padding: .65rem 1rem;
  border: 2px solid rebeccapurple; /* fallback color */
  inline-size: 16ch;               /* fallback width */
  rotate: 0deg;                    /* fallback angle */
}

/* Enhance where typed attr() is supported */
@supports (border-color: attr(data-accent type(<color>))) {
  .chip {
    border-color: attr(data-accent type(<color>), rebeccapurple);
    inline-size: attr(data-w ch, 16ch); /* unitized number → ch */
    rotate: attr(data-rot deg, 0deg); /* number → degrees */
  }
}
```

You can also pull structured types, e.g. `view-transition-name: attr(id type(<custom-ident>), none);`, or accept multiple types: `attr(data-size type(<length> |`

`<percentage>), 24px)`. The key is that casting gives CSS a concrete value it can compute with, not just a string.

Typed `attr()` across properties is Chrome/Edge 133+ today. MDN still marks non-`content` usage as experimental. Gate with `@supports` and provide readable fallbacks.

field-sizing (auto-growing form controls)

`field-sizing` changes how form controls pick their size. With `field-sizing: content`, text inputs, textareas, selects, and file inputs shrinkwrap their content and grow as the user types—the browser does the measuring you used to write JS for. Constrain with `min/max-*` so fields don't collapse or balloon.

```
<label>
  Name
  <input type="text" placeholder="Theo Soti">
</label>

<label>
  Comment
  <textarea rows="1">Hi!</textarea>
</label>
```

```
/* One line to enable content-based sizing */
input, textarea {
  field-sizing: content;
}

/* Defensive limits (recommended) */
input {
  min-inline-size: 7ch;
}

textarea {
  min-block-size: 10rem;
  min-inline-size: 20ch;
  max-inline-size: 50ch;
}
```

Text inputs start as wide as their caret or placeholder and grow until hitting your max and textareas expand inline, then add rows.

Shipping in Chrome/Edge (see the Chrome docs). MDN lists it as limited availability and experimental, with other engines in progress. Use as progressive enhancement and keep sane `min`/`max` guards.

20

Closing Thoughts

We've explored how many common UI patterns and effects can be built today without heavy JavaScript. Smooth scrolling, modals, accordions, carousels, animations, form validation... features that once meant writing dozens of lines of script are now possible with just HTML and CSS.

The guiding idea hasn't changed: **use the least powerful tool that gets the job done**. By leaning on semantics and native browser behavior first, you get performance, accessibility, and simplicity almost for free. CSS has grown into a language capable of handling interactivity and motion that would have seemed impossible a few years ago.

This doesn't mean leaving JavaScript behind. It still shines where it always has: data fetching, application logic, dynamic state. But when you reach for it, it should be intentional. Not because "that's how it's always done," but because it truly adds value.

As browsers evolve, the set of things you don't need JavaScript for will only grow. Staying curious and keeping up with these changes ensures you're building sites that are lighter, more resilient, and kinder to both users and devices.

So the next time you sit down to solve a problem, take a moment before writing your script. Ask yourself: Can HTML and CSS already do this?

You might be surprised how often the answer is yes.

A Short Checklist

1. Can semantics + CSS handle it? If yes, do that.
2. If not, can a native element or attribute get you 80% there?
3. If you add JS, is it necessary, small, and resilient?
4. Do you have graceful fallbacks and accessibility covered?
5. Did you measure the impact (bundle size, CLS/LCP, battery/CPU)?

Build with the least power necessary, and let the platform do the heavy lifting.

Get in Touch

Have a question, found a typo, or want to suggest an improvement? I'd love to hear from you! Email me at `hey@theosoti.com`

Need help with your CSS or website project? I'm available for freelance work. Let's work together, just reach out!

Want to keep learning more about modern CSS and web design? Check out `theosoti.com` for articles, code examples, and updates.

Index

Symbols

:has() **3**
- browser support 9

:has() use cases **3**
- adjacent siblings, checking 7
- advanced combinations 5, 6
- conditional style for navigation 4, 5
- form input style 4
- layouts, changing with toggle 7

A

anchor() function **126**
- tooltip, associating 126
- tooltip, placing with 127
- width, matching 128 – 130

attr() function **142**

B

backdrop
- styling 26, 27

C

CSS Motion Path **71**
- accessibility 77
- aligning 74
- animating, along with curve 75
- container match, with SVG dimensions 73
- HTML structure 71, 72
- optional path visibility 76, 77
- route, drawing 72, 73
- square, drawing 74
- troubleshooting 78, 79

CSS carousel **131**
- navigation arrows, adding 135, 136
- pagination dots, adding 133, 134
- track, layouting 132

CSS form validation **91**
- base styling 93
- coloring, by user states 93
- hidden message list 93
- HTML structure 92
- messages, showing for both classic and user validity 94
- validate, on submit 94, 95

CSS masks effects **81**
- accessibility 85
- complementary masks 83, 84
- divider, updating with JavaScript 85
- grid, for stacking 82, 83
- HTML structure 81, 82
- masked banner silhouette 87, 88
- read-only stars rating 86, 87
- slider, styling 84, 85
- use cases 86

Customizable Select model
- arrow, customizing 118
- button face, styling 117
- clean label 120
- dropdown and options, styling 119, 120
- HTML Structure 116
- opting in 117
- selected option and checkmark, styling 121 – 123

clipping
- avoiding, with fallbacks 127

content animation **32, 33**

counter
- printing 51

custom arrow
- with :after pseudo-element 32

custom border animations
- animatable property, declaring 60
- border layer, adding 59

card, preparing 58
glow, adding 62
gradient, drawing 60
HTML structure 58
reduced motion, respecting 63, 64
spin, animating 61

custom property animation
keyframes count 50
making 50

D

default content
displaying, with open attribute 30

default triangle
hiding 31

dialog
animating 25, 26
opening, with JavaScript 25

F

field-sizing **143**

find-in-page support **31**

fixed header
Global offset 20
handling 20
Per-element offset 21, 22

H

HTML Structure **24**

horizontal scroll **102, 103**

I

Item Flow **140**
masonry-style layout 140

if() function
inline conditionals 140

image reveal section **103, 104**

inline conditionals
with if() function 140

item animation **39, 40**

L

light-dark() function **13, 14**

M

masonry-style layout
via Item Flow 140

mixins **139**

multiple accordions
linking, with name 30

N

Native custom functions **139**

native behaviors **34**

nested sub-headings
numbering 46, 47

P

Popover API
animation, adding 109, 110
built-in close control 109
HTML structure 108
off-canvas menu 111, 112
ordinary CSS, adding 108

pseudo-element
animation, defining 101
animation, linking 101
filling bar, adding 101
fixed background, drawing 100

R

random() function **141**

reduced motion **52**

S

SVG dimensions **73**

System Preference
detecting 12, 13

semantic HTML **29**

sibling-count() function **141**

sibling-index() function **141**

slider container **39**

smooth scrolling **19**
in scrollable containers 20

T

tooltip

placing, with anchor() function 127

top-level headings
numbering 45

U

User Toggle
adding 14, 15

users choice
persisting, with localStorage 16, 17

users control
pausing, on Focus 41, 42
pausing, on Hover 41, 42

V

View Transitions **65**
animation content, selecting 67
HTML structure 66
motion, defining 68
snapshots, styling 67
transitions, activating 67

variations and styles **48**

www.ingramcontent.com/pod-product-compliance
Lightning Source LLC
LaVergne TN
LVHW060038210926
848481LV00013B/3896
9781807783419